Edit Like You Stole It

Edit Like You Stole It

Even a moron like me can line edit

Tim Girsby

First edition 2024

Cover © Stuart Bache 2024

ISBN 978-1-7384702-0-4 (paperback)
ISBN 978-1-7384702-1-1 (ebook)

Published by Idiot Machine Publishing
idiotmachinepublishing.com

Contents

Preface

A terrible admission of idiocy

I didn't mean to write this book.

I thought I was writing pretty well. I'd got a solid second draft of my fantasy novel (started over lockdown, natch) and I was putting together an unrelated second book. However, I'd joined a critique circle, and some of the folks there were pulling me apart for basic stuff – passive voice, hand-wavy descriptions, weak verbs, shallow characters. I realised I needed to level up. So, I set out to teach myself to line edit fiction.

There's a trick that Richard Feynman used to use when he wanted to learn something. Who's Richard Feynman? Oh, he's just, you know, a guy who had a Nobel prize for discovering a load of the most important bits of science ever, that's who. His technique for learning was simple. First; read about it. Easy! Go and buy a book or watch a video or whatever works for you. Step one, done! Now, step two: you must teach it to someone.

Wait, what?

Yes, that's right. The idea here is that you explain what you've learnt to someone else. And ideally, it's a real person, and you're really teaching this to them for the first time. Not everyone does this: sometimes they might just talk to their dog or stuffed toy or house plant or poltergeist, safe in the knowledge that they won't make themselves look a fool.

But this, friends, is not the spirit of the game.

So, here we are. I learnt by reading a lot of blogs and books. I played with stuff, where I tried to edit my own text in a rather more disciplined way. I read things with a really critical eye. I asked questions of people who are better than me, including some who are trad published, and others who are successful self-published authors.

Then I down wrote what I learnt. I engaged Feynman mode: I published a chapter a week on Wattpad, and people piled in and told me what was wrong (and also what was right, which was gratifying).

And then I took it to the next level! I got an actual professional editor to look at it, and she sighed and told me what to fix (actually, she didn't, she's lovely), and I edited it again and again, adding and cutting... And here you are, holding the finished product in your hands.

I think that this is the core stuff you need to know to be a fiction writer, down at the line edit level. There is loads more to learn, because writing is amazing, and the subtleties of it are endless, so you should see this a place to jump from, not a place to stop.

And, yeah, you guessed it. I'm still learning. When you've finished, tell me what's wrong, tell me what's right, tell me what's missing! I'm on Wattpad and Substack as theidiotmachine. Come say hi.

Now, let's begin!

Introduction

Edit like you stole it!

This book is called *Edit Like You Stole It* for two reasons.

The first is that it made me laugh. In my defence, by the time I got to the stage where I needed a title I'd slogged through I don't know how many revisions and my sense of humour had worn pretty thin.

The second, though, and the reason that this title stuck, is that there's nothing new in fiction. Nothing at all. I don't know when the new stuff stopped being created. I've heard a suggestion that it was in the golden age of science fiction in the sixties. That seems far too recent: perhaps when the original printing presses filled the world with chapbooks they used up the last of humanity's novelty reserves. More likely, though, I think all the original ideas were dreamt up when we told each other stories around fires, tens of thousands of years ago.

So when we write fiction everything is stolen. A lot of it

is taken unconsciously, just from dipping into of our shared understanding of language and plot and structure; but the rest of the theft is premeditated. We see an idea and decide to cleverly reframe it in a way that we think might surprise and delight our readers. We imagine a character as a composite of two others. We set a familiar plot in a different environment. We distort and change and twist, but the things we start with are not ours.

There's nothing wrong with this. Every scene, every phrase, every face and prop and reveal, they can't all be new. But it doesn't matter.

From a certain point of view, it doesn't matter because your readers haven't read all fiction, so they might not know that you didn't invent it all.

But, less cynically, no one is expecting everything to be unique. It's true that your readers don't want your work to be a lazy knock-off, a piece obviously derivative of something else. But they're also expecting the tropes of fiction, the grooves and tunnels and hollows worn smooth with age, the familiar landscape of storytelling which has been with us for as long as language has. Oh yes: as a writer you're now a custodian of the very oldest and finest art-form which humanity possesses. Look after it.

But if nothing is new, what's the point? Why bother? And the answer is simple: because your work will mean something to someone. It will bring a brightness to a life, and that might be the most worthwhile thing anyone can do.

I think of writing as both an art and a craft. The art is the idea and the form. The craft is the skill of storytelling, of weaving a world from nothing but words. This craft has many branches, but the most obvious is that of putting one word after another, of laying down sentences to paragraphs to sections to chapters to books, and having every one of them be perfect. And the art may be borrowed, repurposed, an echo of a thousand similar things, but that doesn't mean the craft should be shoddy. At the end, no one should be able to see the seams, the places where we attached this idea to that to make a thing which is not quite new, but maybe not so old, either. And the place where we fix those joins, smooth over everything so that it is a single, perfect entity, is the edit.

I know nothing about sculpture and it shows

When we say 'the edit,' what, exactly, are we talking about?

There are three major types or phases of editing. They are developmental editing, copy editing (which includes line editing) and proof reading. You should think of them as being at different scales: I like to imagine that, if you are a sculptor, a development edit is like using a sledgehammer, a copy edit is like using a chisel, and a proof read is like using sandpaper. I will not lie, I'm not completely sure that sculptors use sledgehammers, but I'm not here to discuss sculpting and know nothing about it, so I'm going to pass over that in silence. I promise this will make sense in a minute.

So what does that analogy mean from an actual, you know, useful perspective?

Development editing is large scale, structural editing. You're going to move sections around, delete chunks, slim bits down, and bulk other parts up. You're looking at overall character journeys, pace, and tone. You're checking that every Chekhov's gun has been fired, that every plot event grew from a previously planted seed, that there is just the right amount of exposition to understand what's going on. You might delete a character, or scene, or split one into two, or merge two into one. You might even change substantial parts of your plot. You'll often spend the most time here, because manuscripts generally require multiple developmental edits. At the end, you'll end up with great characterisations, points-of-view, voices, settings, and plot arcs.

Generally it's the first edit you do. I'm terrible at it, and I hate it, so you're on your own. All I can say is: take it easy, be kind to yourself. Yes, it can feel bad changing or removing things you worked so hard on in the first place, but you'll end up with a better book. When you cut big chunks of stuff, put it in a file. Keep them, and read them later – you're free to steal from your past self.

In my sculpting analogy, maybe development editing is more like using a chainsaw and superglue. Don't like the pose of the left arm? Cut it off, jam it back on better.

Once you've really got the structure right, next is the copy edit. And, yeah, you really do need to get the big stuff nailed first. Copy editing before you've properly got your developmental edits done isn't a recipe for disaster so much as a recipe for redoing lots of work, which is irritating.

So, now that you're happy with the whole flow of your story, you need to make every sentence beautiful. This is, I think, the best bit. Why? Because you're letting your prose breathe. You had all these amazing ideas. You got them down. Well done! You read it all, realised that it needed changing, and so you moved some stuff around and deleted the text which didn't move the story along. Even more well done! And now, it's time to make every dang word shine.

This is the bit that's gonna make your readers jump for

joy, when every word stands out like a spark in the darkness, and the prose flows effortlessly. It takes a long time. All the littles curve of Michelangelo's David needs to be chiselled out, including his butt. But, I promise you, it's going to be fun.

Yes, I totally said butt there. My book, my rules.

There are two parts to the copy editing. There's making sure all your capitalisation and punctuation and spelling is correct. This is, frankly, dull as hell. I'm not going to teach you that because manuals are everywhere and also, I'm terrible at it. No, the thing I want to teach you is line editing, which is the creative part of copy editing. As I said, if the original writing is the art, line editing and development editing are part of the craft. It's what lifts your ideas to gleaming perfection.

Lastly we get to proof reading. Here someone reads your whole manuscript from cover to cover, looking for stuff missed by everyone else. You do that last because, if you're like me, in the edit phases you delete a closing quotation mark, or you type *is* instead of *it*, or you're inconsistent with some spelling or other. This is where you pick these little mistakes up, and make the whole thing look professional. This is the sanding: it is meticulous work, but it removes the last rough edges.

In this book I present you one bite-sized lesson on line editing per chapter. Each one contains a thing to look out for, and what to do about it. I hate guides that just shout rules at you, though, so I've tried to be very clear about why we're doing these things, and what happens if you don't.

Although it's all very cheerful and breezy, there's a lot of technical stuff to digest here. Take notes, highlight stuff, if you're using Feynman's technique, prepare whatever you need to teach someone! I tried to make it easy to use as a reference: every chapter has a summary at the end, so you can jump straight to that when you're refreshing your memory, and where I could, I made the chapter names stupid jokes that remind you of what the core issues are. I also made sure that you could read some of my sources and other stuff that I liked, in the further reading sections.

When I published this on Wattpad I dropped a chapter or two a week: as a result, my beta readers read it as a serial, and went away and did something else in between. This might be a good technique to emulate. But if you want to gobble the whole thing up in one go, well, maybe that works too.

A lot of this book is about 'show, don't tell.' As a writer you've heard this before, and it's comically terrible advice given the actual phrase 'show, don't tell' tells and doesn't show. As we'll see, in line editing this mantra is not one thing: it's actually a group of unrelated guidelines. These include 'action rather than summary,' 'objective rather than subjective,' and 'dialogue that doesn't need adverbs' and a lot of other little things.

Oh, there is one golden rule to bear in mind. This rule is that all books about not making mistakes when you write have mistakes in them. Let me know what you find.

Onwards!

Chapter 1

The shark yodelled grammar at us

Meet your new grammar friends

Hey! Before we really get going, I'm going to give you a brief refresher on some grammar. Don't freak out: it's actually easy. Some people are really frightened of grammar, and I get why, it's all complicated terms and hard-to-define concepts. So, I'm going to hold your hand through this, and remind you of the basics here, and as we go through the book we'll gradually meet some new stuff. You might be able to skip this first chapter if you paid attention at school, but I didn't, so I can't.

The two key things we're going to cover here are verbs and nouns. Understanding those – verbs, in particular – is going to really let us sail through the first few chapters.

A noun is a word which means a person or a thing or stuff. *Balloon, Janet, light, sand,* or more abstract things like *fear* or *boredom,* these are all nouns. When you play 'eye spy', those things that you point at and guess the names of are all nouns.

Verbs are actions; they are changes to the world. So, *write, complain, laugh,* and *fall* are all verbs.

Now, I use the phrase 'show don't tell' an awful lot in the book, and I'm going to live by that mantra, too. So let's show you an example, rather than tell you about it. I'm sure you've seen this before.

> The **shark yodelled**.

Yep, can't get away from those yodelling sharks. *Yodel* is a verb. *Shark* is a noun. I've heard that some people want to try and restrict the yodelling to certain hours, and I get it, but I think it's sweet and the sharks should be free to sing when they like.

Let's try another one.

> **Janet smiled**, and **patted** the **shark**. It **wriggled**, and then **yodelled** some more.

There are loads of verbs and nouns here! The verbs are *smiled, patted, wriggled,* and *yodelled,* because those are 'action' words. The nouns are *Janet* and *shark,* because those are 'thing' words. Then *it* is a pronoun, and we'll look at pronouns in chapter five so you can forget about that for the moment.

The key thing to get from this chapter is that you can pick out a verb in a line-up. We're going to see a lot of them to start with.

Because, at the end of the day, all writing is just verbs and nouns. Yes, there are other, fancier things too, and we will look at them all, but actually, these two simple parts of grammar are the nuts and bolts of our craft. They are the girders that hold everything up.

Now that we've covered this, the next few chapters will easy. So, let's go.

Chapter 2

I realised I was filtering

You saw the filter

Filtering is like those stereogram things. Do you know the ones that I mean? They're a page of seemingly randomly coloured pixels. You kind of stare at them a bit boss-eyed, and suddenly a three-dimensional shape jumps out at you. After that, you can do them, they just always work, and you can never unsee them.

Well, once you can see filtering, that's you, too – although seeing filtering is something of a curse, because it's rarely welcome and we want to cut it. But, like a stereogram, filtering is easier to show than to explain.

So, here's an example. This is from a deeply touching scene. Our main character, Janet, has just killed the evil Slicken von Klicken, and is sitting on her jet-ski in the supermarket car park.

> Janet **felt** the cold wind on her, and **saw** the empty plastic bags as they danced over the tarmac. **She could sense** the exhaustion creeping up on her, the tension draining from her body. The birds **were waking**, and **she could hear** their calls around her. The rhinoceroses crept from their tunnels, snorting to each other in the early morning sun. **She watched**, silently, as they waltzed together across the empty car park, and **listened** to the thunder of their feet on the ground.
>
> **She thought** how happy they looked.

Is that so bad, you might be asking yourself? Well, maybe.

Filtering is like I'm picking up a sheet of coloured plastic, and I'm putting it on top of the scene. I'm forcing my reader to see the world through this colour, rather than using their own eyes. By doing that I'm pushing them a little away from the experience. At the same time, I'm slowing the pace down by padding it out with words I don't need, often with weak verbs which are imprecise and don't make us dance with delight. This is a theme we'll keep coming back to, by the way: weak verbs are our enemy.

Well okay. But what's the filter?

The filter is the perceptions of the main character, Janet. I'm filtering the book's descriptions through her, and I don't need to. When Janet felt the cold wind, it's not necessary to say that it was Janet feeling it. It's enough to describe that the wind was cold, because as a reader we sit pretty close to our protagonist, sometimes in their mind, sometimes a little outside. What they see, we see.

Writing it out explicitly is redundant.

Filtering is a good place to start this book, because if you have it, it can mean one of two things. The first is nice and easy: it's just a thing you've never noticed before. If that's the case, well, great! Finding out about it is one of those lightbulb moments for new writers, we've all been there, welcome to the club, it's good to have you.

The second thing it can mean is that you've not figured your character out yet. You haven't quite stepped into their mind, so when you write you're a little removed from them. There are a few other symptoms of this, too, which we'll look at later in the book, in chapter eleven on point of view.

This is true for me: in my first novel one of my protagonists was perfectly crystallised in my mind, and the other wasn't. When I wrote the weaker one's sections I sort of skirted around his point of view, and filtering is definitely one of those ways to skirt. Remember when I said in the introduction, about how you need to finish the developmental editing first? Yes, this is that. A deep, well-drawn cast of characters is vital to avoid filtering.

But I'm sure you've sorted your characters, and I'm just being a silly old worrier! And, anyway, that's not really a line edit thing. So, instead, let's talk about how we can remove filtering.

We'll go back to my example, and look at the first sentence. Here it is, so you don't have to flip back.

> Janet **felt** the cold wind on her, **saw** the empty plastic bags as they danced over the tarmac.

Remember that filtering is needlessly creating space between the reader's and character's perceptions, by experiencing the world through a character. It generally manifests as a particular set of verbs: here they are *felt* and *saw*. They are boring, imprecise, and they are pushing us away from our character's perceptions. So, let's think how we could rewrite this sentence.

I think I would do something like this.

> The cold wind **sliced** into Janet's exposed fingers and face. It **whirled** the empty plastic bags over the tarmac.

This is actually slightly longer than the original, but I prefer it. I've used two separate techniques, and they're both things we'll see more of later.

The first is to lean in, and decide that the cold wind is a thing that it's important for us to know that Janet is experiencing. So, I've beefed up the verb. It's no longer *feel*, it's now *slice*, which is not an experience verb, so I'm describing the same thing and being less wishy-washy from filtering.

The second is to take Janet away from the sentence completely. We don't need to know that she's seeing something, because we see what she sees: let's just remove that. It meant I had to find another new verb, because now we're directly describing the world, and I chose *whirl* which is nice, because *dance* can't really be used in that slot.

Good! Back to my passage. Here's the rest of that first paragraph.

Can you see the filtering, now? You can do it!

> She could **sense** the exhaustion creeping up on her, the tension draining from her body. The birds were waking, and she could **hear** their calls around her. The rhinoceroses crept from their tunnels, snorting to each other in the early morning sun. She **watched**, silently, as they waltzed together across the empty car park, **listened** to the thunder of their feet on the ground.

Yes, there it is. *Sense, hear, watched* and *listened* are all filter verbs. Let's rewrite the whole caboodle to fix this.

> The tension **drained** from her, the exhaustion **rising** like a tide. The birds were waking, **calling** to each other. The rhinoceroses crept from their tunnels, snorting to each other in the early morning sun. They met, and then **waltzed** together across the empty car park, their feet **thundering** on the ground.

Again, the two techniques. For the tension and exhaustion, I've decided that it's important to show that this is a thing that Janet is experiencing, so I've leaned in: I've replaced *sense* with a much more impactful verb. I kept *drain* because, actually, that's quite nice.

For the rest, it's much easier: it's pretty mechanical, I just deleted the filter sections and then cleaned up the sentence. All my verbs are nice, punchy, non-filter verbs. In those sentences, those verbs were always there, hiding in tunnels like the rhinos, I've just given them space to waltz.

Importantly, when you read it now, you're not distracted by looking at yourself. Remember, 'you' is Janet, because that's who your protagonist is. You're looking at the dancing pachyderms, not at yourself in the jet-ski wing mirror. Oh, and if you've never seen a rhino waltz, seriously, you've missed nothing. They've got two left feet.

Getting rid of some filtering is harder than others. Let's try this one. If you remember, this is the immediate next sentence.

> She **thought** how happy they looked.

Filtering, eh? Yeah, you can see it now. We're showing the world through Janet, when the world is already experienced through her.

However, *thought* is different from *saw* or *heard*. There's an important reason for that. To illustrate that, let's first treat it the same way we did the last two sentences, and cut out the filter words.

> They looked so happy.

This is clearly simpler, but it misses the nuance of the original. When Janet was just looking at the rhinos dance, we didn't lose anything when we cut away the filter words. But when we saw *thought* we're being told that this is a thing that she thinks about, and presumably cares about.

What I'm doing with this kind of filtering, using words like *thought*, is summarising her inner thoughts.

Now, one version of 'show, don't tell' is 'write out fully, don't summarise.' Summarising can be a useful tool if we want to hurry the plot along, but it introduces a level of distance between us and the action that can be very unsatisfactory if overused. I think about this like driving: when I'm in a low gear I want to luxuriate in my character's opinions and wants. When I'm in a high gear skipping boring things, well, a bit of summary lets me crank out the plot at speed.

When you find these kind of filtered, summarised thoughts, it's worth trying to drop down a gear into direct thought, and seeing whether it gets bogged down much. If it's still fast enough, you gain a bit of intimacy for free by switching.

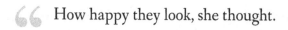 How happy they look, she thought.

Now, we're in a deep point of view. We're inside her head as the thoughts are occurring. We've stripped away another layer of narrative, and we get to be closer to her as she experiences the world.

When not to delete filtering with cavalier abandon

Okay, by now you hopefully know what filtering is, why we want to get rid of it, and how to do that. Maybe, you ain't buying it.

Look, I get it. It feels like you're making the text poorer; you're stripping away some of the nuance of the characters. And the reality is, you are. So... whisper it... filtering isn't all bad. Here are three and a half times that you should think a bit before stripping out filtering words.

1) Filtering isn't filtering when it's not your viewpoint character doing the looking, it's some other character. You're not in their brain, so let them look around as much as they like!

> Janet picked up her gun, and put it into its holster. She clicked the cover closed. Satisfied, she limped over to Sally, who was sitting slumped against the base of the ticket machine.
>
> Sally met her gaze, and then **looked** away, exhaustion stamped into her expression.

We're still in Janet's head, so Sally can look at what she wants, this isn't filtering. I would note that your viewpoint character conventionally cannot see into other people's minds, so although they can follow where they're looking, they can't properly experience what this third-party smells or hears or realizes. It's also... maybe... a bit boring recounting what other people are looking at? We'll cover this in stage directions, in chapter sixteen. This also leaks into head-hopping, which we will cover later in chapter twelve.

2) When the actual focus of the sentence is the filter verb, you need to be careful about how you cut it.

> Janet sat down next to Sally. Her back ached and her left leg throbbed.
>
> She took a deep breath, and **realised** that she **could smell** lavender.

'My nose is working again,' she said.

The *realised* and *could smell* are filter words. However, we aren't just showing the world through her: her experiencing a sense is important to our understanding of the text. Contrast with this, where I've given it the standard filter removal treatment.

> Janet sat down next to Sally. Her back ached and her left leg throbbed dully.
>
> She took a deep breath. The scent of lavender wafted down from the trees behind her.
>
> 'My nose is working again,' she said.

It reads more nicely, but we've lost emphasis from the critical detail: her realisation that she's regained her sense of smell. This is tricky; filtering verbs are boring, which means removing it is generally the right thing to do, so you'll need to make a call about how to resolve that. A deeper restructure might be the right solution. Here's mine:

> Janet sat down next to Sally. Her back ached and her left leg throbbed dully.
>
> She took a deep breath. The scent of lavender flooded into her nose.
>
> 'Hey, I just realised: I can smell again,' she said.

I pushed the work of the filter into dialogue, so we find out about her realisation when she tells Sally. If there's no one around to talk to, because Sally is fighting the robot minions on another continent, then *realised* is a great candidate to turn from summary into direct thought. I think the technique is always this: ask yourself what you're telling the reader about your character's experiences. What are more engaging ways of showing it than using filtering words?

3) If you're in a first-person point of view, your protagonist's thoughts will leak into the text. Filter words look very much like inner monologue words. This is from a different story:

> As I scrambled down the slope, the king penguin's words rang in my ears: the Brotherhood of Yetis were not to be trusted. I **saw** that my snowmobile was where I'd left it, the cold winds roaring around me, the snow piling up. I climbed on, and **considered** my options as I roared away across the ice.
>
> In the end I **decided** to keep my end of the bargain; I didn't **think** they'd double cross me. There were only so many flower shops in Antarctica, after all, and making them disappear would cause them problems with the walruses.
>
> I smiled to myself, and **imagined** the look on Mrs Miggins's face when I gave her the Final Fragrant Icicle.

This is much trickier than when we were in third person! The first filter, *saw*, I definitely should get rid of. When

13

we're in first person, we're right in someone's head, and they're either recounting a story to us, or we're living it through them. As a reminder, this is what it looked like.

> I **saw** that my snowmobile was where I'd left it, [...]

This is classic redundant filtering. We can fix it very easily.

> The snowmobile was where I'd left it, [...]

It means exactly the same, while saving myself a couple of words.

The others are more complicated. The narrator is talking to us conversationally, and so this is less like true filtering, and much more like speech. However, if you look closely, you can see that what I'm doing here with those filter verbs is summarising his thoughts, and that's getting between us and him.

Here's a version without that.

> As I scrambled down the slope, the king penguin's words rang in my ears: the Brotherhood of Yetis were not to be trusted. My snowmobile was where I'd left it, the cold winds roaring around me, the snow piling up. I climbed on, and roared away across the ice.
>
> What was I going to do?
>
> There were only so many flower shops in Antarctica, and the yetis couldn't just make

them all disappear without causing problems with the walruses, so double crossing me would be hard. On balance, keeping my end of the bargain would make sense.

I smiled to myself. Mrs Miggin's face was going to light up like a Christmas tree when I gave her the Final Fragrant Icicle.

It's longer, but it's also much more immediate. That's because I've exploited the way that in first person the narrative leaks into inner thoughts; the filtering was summarising these thoughts, and by removing it, I've been forced to write them out fully.

Now, as we said, maybe you just want to get on, in which case a bit of gentle summarising is the right thing to do. But balance your reader's desire to move the plot with their need to get closer to the character.

3 ½) The three-and-a-half reason to think a bit more carefully about filtering is that a bit of gentle seeing and hearing can help with point of view establishment. This is only half a reason because I'm not going to cover it here, we'll look at this properly in the point of view chapter, chapter twelve; but remember the thing I keep hammering on about: filtering is boring. Using it is last resort stuff.

Summary

I promised you a summary at the end of every chapter. If you've read the book all the way through and are returning to it for reference, hi! This is for you. It's good to see you, it's been a while, I hope you're well.

Filtering is when we dilute our reader's experiences through our characters' perceptions. Filtering verbs are things like *saw, heard, sensed, knew.* They are weak, imprecise, and bog the text down, so we generally don't want to filter.

For mundane experience verbs, we delete the filtering verb. Those are words like:

Saw, watched, looked at, could see, spotted.
Heard, could hear, listened to.
Touched, felt, could feel.
Smelt, could smell.
Tasted, could taste.
Sensed, experienced, could sense.
Seemed to.
So,

 She **watched** the giant unicycle explode.

Becomes:

 The giant unicycle exploded.

For thought filter verbs, we go deeper into our character's experience, by unpacking summarisation of thoughts into direct thoughts. We do that for words like these:

Noticed, realised, discovered, remembered, wondered, believed, knew, thought.

 He remembered to pick up soul bread.

Becomes:

16

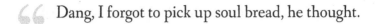 Dang, I forgot to pick up soul bread, he thought.

Although removing filtering tends to be a no-brainer to improve our prose, there are some times we need to be careful.

1) When the filter verb is actually not filtering, because it's not the viewpoint character doing it.

Janet followed Sally's gaze: she was **looking** at the uranium circlet. It was about to explode.

This is a stage direction, and we look at them later.

2) When the character experiencing something is key to our understanding of the text.

As the fog cleared, she **noticed** that the goat was laughing at her.

How could I be so stupid, she thought. Of course. The goat was working for the enemy all along.

We think hard about whether we can restructure to remove the filter verb, without losing the key information.

3) In first person point of view, filtering verbs are harder to unpick, because of the nature of the narrative. As with third, though, they can be just mundane filtering, or they can be an indication that we're summarising thought.

> I ran my fingers over the signpost. It **seemed** to crackle. I **wondered** if they really had turned off the power.

Seemed is true filtering and can be removed; *wondered* is a summary of thought, and can be expanded, if we think it's worth it.

4) If you really must, filtering can be used to establish point of view, but it's boring, so try not to.

Further reading

Scribophile is a website where you can find other people to critique your work. It's really great. It also has some useful resources in its Writing Academy. This is where I first learnt about filtering. https://www.scribophile.com/academy/an-introduction-to-filtering

Louise Harnby's blog is incredible and always worth reading. I really like how deep she goes here. https://www.louiseharnbyproofreader.com/blog/filter-words-in-fiction-purposeful-inclusion-and-dramatic-restriction

September C. Fawkes is another editor with a fantastic blog. Here's her take. https://www.septembercfawkes.com/2018/02/breaking-writing-rules-right-dont-use.html

Chapter 3

I started to begin

Stop starting

Are you constantly starting projects and not finishing them? Beginning and not ending? Do you have a stash of half-cooked works on your hard drive or in the cloud?

Yeah, me too! It's one of the reasons I like writing short fiction. But I'm not here to castigate you about that; I'm here to talk about something completely different. In this chapter we're going to discuss the words *start* and *begin*.

It's a nice short one. I'm going to interleave the easier chapters with the harder ones, so you're not tar pitted on the really nasty stuff in the beginning and give up.

Anyway, the concept here is nice and simple: the words *start* and *begin* are not your friends. Or, at least, not always. Let's use an example.

 The balloon **started** to pop.

The issue here is that started is wasting your reader's time. You're just padding. The balloon will pop pretty much instantaneously, so don't bother telling us it started. By the end of the sentence, it's already just bits of plastic in the president's hair.

> The balloon popped.

Much nicer. However, it's often not as obvious as that.

> Hamza **began to brush** his teeth. Outside, the birds **started to sing** to the rising sun.

The reason that I wrote that is because I wanted to show that the two things were happening at the same time, so I showed them starting together. And brushing teeth and birdsong are not instantaneous, so it should be okay to start them, right?

But, actually, it's just word gunk. You almost never need starting or beginning. Try it without:

> Hamza **brushed** his teeth. Outside, the birds **sang** to the rising sun.

It actually hasn't lost anything, right? It's shorter, and therefore punchier, and the two events we described are still happening concurrently: we know that Hamza is standing in front of the mirror while sparrows are hollering in the garden.

So: when you see *start, begin, commence, initiate* or some

similar words, consider excising them.

Perhaps continue starting

Think we're done? Not so fast! There are two valid reasons for keeping these little words in.

The first is that the action never gets finished (like our manuscripts. Ouch). In this case, you have a stronger case for keeping your *start*, because that's all that happened, and removing the word changes the sentence.

> Rheese **began** to turn the wheel, but the hamster kicked him away.

It's still not great, though. One of the reasons that we don't like these words is that they aren't very exciting. Maybe there's a better way.

> Rheese **grabbed** the wheel, but the hamster kicked him away.

Here we replaced the *began* with the actual action he completed before the dastardly hamster put the boot in. Oh, and don't feel too bad for Rheese: he's actually going to spin poor Mr Whisker's wheel without his permission.

The second case is very similar, and that's when the action won't be finished for a long time.

> Isidora sank into her acceleration couch, and buckled herself in. She flicked on the comm.

21

'Control, this is the USS Secateurs. I'm ready.'

'Copy that, Secateurs. Please commence launch checks.'

Isidora nodded, and **started** the starship's fault scan.

'On it, Control. Liang, can you make me a coffee, please? It's going to be a long night.'

In this case, yes, Isidora will be doing various space things for some time. She might stop and have a bite to eat, or she might just slug on and get it done as quickly as she can. Again, though; it's pretty weak, right? Can we turn this into an action that she completes?

" Isidora sank into her acceleration couch, and buckled herself in. She flicked on the comm.

'Control, this is the USS Secateurs. I'm ready.'

'Copy that, Secateurs. Please commence launch checks.'

Isidora nodded, and **ran** the starship's fault scan.

'On it, Control. Liang, can you make me a coffee, please? It's going to be a long night.'

This is only marginally better. Again, we know from all the other cues that the work won't be done immediately, but this time, the *start* wasn't really a problem. It's just a bit dull. How about this:

> Isidora sank into her acceleration couch, and buckled herself in. She flicked on the comm.
>
> 'Control, this is the USS Secateurs. I'm ready.'
>
> 'Copy that, Secateurs. Please commence launch checks.'
>
> Isidora stifled a yawn. 'On it, Control. Liang, can you make me a coffee, please? It's going to be a long night.'

I just nixed it, and honestly, it's fine. Talking about what people do on computers is generally quite boring, it's why writing about hacking is so hard. It just so happened that the verb *start* was one of those computer verbs, and so the fact that it was a long-running action was a red herring. If it's really important to the plot that you understand that the fault scan was started, then maybe you should restructure that sentence some more.

That felt pretty niche, so here's another one.

> The mists swirled around her, and the sky demons shivered and withdrew. As they faded away, their tears collected on the floor, hardening into glass beads.
>
> Nadia knelt, and collected them, whispering the name of each demon as she did so. Their tear beads were so icy that they clung to her fingers. She packed them into her satchel, and when she stood up, they clicked against each other, and the chill leaked through the leather.

> The gate was open now. She bowed one last
> time, turned, and **began** the long walk home.

In this case, yes, she'll be walking for some time home. Nadia might stop and collect some more sky demon tear beads, or she might just keep going. Again though: that *began* is pretty weak, right? Plus the *long walk home* is a cliché.

> The gate was open now. She bowed one last
> time, turned, and walked through. As she did,
> there was one last wild laugh from the storm.

I turned it into a thing that she did, rather than a thing that she started. The rhythm was worse, so I threw in a last sentence to fix it.

For these, playing with them is a good idea. Trying different things is fun and can take you to some surprising places.

Summary

Begin, start, commence: these are all weak words.

Generally you'll remove them, because the verb they refer to is quite happy without them.

Sometimes, it's important to indicate that an action was started, because it was abandoned, or won't be completed for some time: however, ask yourself if you could still show a smaller completed action rather than an uncompleted one, because that tends to be more immediate and therefore more satisfying.

Chapter 4

Fragments are so

Grammar refresher with our friends the octopus and shark

Fragments. I just can't even. I really can't. But you? You could, right?

I'll stop now! It's irritating even me and I'm the one writing it. But hopefully, you get the idea: in this chapter, we're talking about sentence fragments.

In order to understand what a sentence fragment is, we need to remind ourselves of a tiny bit of grammar. Don't run away! It's easy, I promise.

Earlier we looked at what verbs and nouns are. Well, according to classical grammar, a sentence contains at least one noun and one verb. The thing we didn't talk about before is that verbs have a few different slots that nouns can sit in, and those slots have different names.

Let's look at an example.

> **The octopus laughed**.

We've said that *laughed* is a verb and *octopus* is a noun, but what we've not said is that *octopus* is being used as the 'subject.' The subject is the noun that the sentence is about, hence the name. It's, generally, what's doing the action indicated by the verb, and in this case, yes, the octopus is indeed doing the laughing.

Great. Let's look at a slightly longer example.

> **The shark ignored** the **octopus**.

Okay. There are two nouns here, *shark* and *octopus*, and one verb, *ignored*. The octopus is overtired, and she's being silly, and the shark is very much being the mature one here. Now, the subject is the shark, because she's the one doing the ignoring: we call the other noun the 'object' and that's the one that the verb is being done to, and that's the octopus. We have to have a verb to make a sentence, and the verb has to have a subject, and this particular verb needs an object (*the shark ignored* doesn't make a lot of sense) so we have that too.

By the way, I say 'according to classical grammar,' but actually grammar is a bit more permissive: there's a case for various short speech parts to be complete sentences on their own, most famously *no*. If you Google 'no is a complete sentence' you'll get lots of self-help stuff about boundaries, and some grumpy grammar blogs picking fights.

An important class of things that can live on their own are the 'interjections.' These are things like people swearing, sound effects, and fillers. So, this extremely short story is actually made of complete sentences:

> Um...
>   Kablooie!
>   Dang.

So, when we're talking about fragments, we'll worry about classical sentences, ones with verbs in them. However, overuse of interjections is irritating, and actually, a lot of what I'm going to talk about here covers those too.

Great. If you look up right now, you'll see some gold stars falling around you. That's because you just levelled up at grammar. Now, let's get to the actual issue.

Spitting shards

When you omit the various necessary parts of a classical sentence, you've made a fragment. We actually saw one earlier.

> The shark ignored.

This is pretty obviously wrong, and you wouldn't write something like this. We'll see stickier issues later, though.

Unlike our previous topics, fragments are less stylistic choice and more skating over the frozen abyss of incorrectness. You know this, because your editing software may put a blue squiggly line under it, with the note 'fragment: consider revising.' We're going to look at what's okay and what's not, and we'll talk about what to keep and what you should fix.

First off, dialogue. Have you ever read a transcript of normal people talking? Not of a pre-planned, rehearsed speech, but just humans sharing information with other humans using their fleshy breathing holes. It's amazing. It's ungrammatical, it's riddled with repetition and fillers, and most of all, it's all fragments. It's easy to listen to and exhausting to read.

When we write dialogue in fiction we don't write what people really say, otherwise our most commonly used words would be *er* and *um*. We don't want to tax our readers. We write what our characters intend to say, not what they would actually say in reality.

What this means, though, is that dialogue is one of the places where fragments are more acceptable. However, they have a specific meaning: our characters are unable to form whole sentences because there is something significant preventing them from doing so. It might be an emotional state such as grief or surprise, it might be a physical state such as exhaustion.

> Colin the polar bear crashed into the room, broken photocopier in tow.
>
> Sheena was on the phone, trying to talk someone through an installation of Windows 98. Colin waved cheerfully and sent a pile of modems tumbling.
>
> **'I'm not... It's not...** Can't you just turn it off and on again?' she asked, as beige plastic boxes smashed around her and their circuit board innards span across the storeroom floor.
>
> Colin winced.

Here, ellipses show that the fragment is caused by speech tailing off. Fragments and ellipses tend to accompany each other, because they help you understand what has been omitted; in this case, our speaker tried to start three sentences and only succeeded at the last one.

Now, as I said, in reality everyone talks like this all the time. However, in fiction it has a particular meaning: it shows that extreme emotion prevented a speaker from speaking properly, maybe pain or despair. In Sheena's case, it's because she's distracted and irritated by a polar bear in a striped one-piece bathing suit, who's destroying everything in her storeroom. Plus, he's late again. Oh, Colin.

I said that fragments are bad, but this use is okay. I'm using them judiciously, and because we know how people speak, our tolerance for fragments in dialogue is rather higher than in other places. Still, if you had loads of them, your dialogue would start feeling choppy.

'Let her... One last time...'

The old man's breathing was hoarse and shallow. Sunil's medical scanner bleeped once: there was nothing he could do to save him.

'Must... Remember... Topiary...'

Isidora put her hand on his arm. She blinked away the tears.

'I'm so... I'm so sorry...'

I think this is going too far, and the whole trope of panting out fragments as you die is such a cliché anyway. Yes, people say fragments, but it's not what we enjoy reading. And, actually, this isn't how people speak, either: try reading it aloud. It sounds horribly artificial.

I'd edit this to have everyone say whole sentences.

When we use fragments, they make our reader work harder. Our brains can't get full context from the current sentence, so they have to search a bit further afield to make sense of what's going on. I think fragments are well named, because it's almost like when you're cleaning, and you find little shards of glass. Sure, you can sweep them into your dustpan, but you're a bit careful because you don't want to cut yourself, and it slows you down. So, even though transcribed speech is full of fragments, we write full sentences in fiction because they're easier to read.

We keep fragments in dialogue for special occasions.

Where things are acceptable in speech, they're also acceptable in a first-person point of view.

> I stumbled into the room, coughing from the green smoke.
>
> Oh, no. This wasn't possible. **Couldn't be**. I'd checked. **All the ingredients, every one of them**. **And yet... And yet**. Mrs Miggins was now a vampire. Whoops...

First person often dips between narration and inner thoughts, and when you're in the latter, fragments give the same distracted, frantic feel as they do in dialogue. Note how I went pretty light on the ellipses. If you put those three little dots on the end of every fragment it looks just horrible. You may remember that *oh, no* and *whoops* aren't fragments:

they're interjections, but they add to the confused atmosphere. It's why I said that even if interjections are not true fragments, you need to treat them with the same care.

Here, you're paying a cost. I argue, without any kind of scientific basis, that part of the frantic, stressful feel from fragments is your mind doing extra work. It's exhausting, so you should use them very, very judiciously. Make sure your fragments are punchy and only used at key points, and if they aren't, consider whether you should make them full sentences, or delete them.

Nouns on the Run

There's another fragment that I personally hate, but I know some writers use. This is the noun phrase fragment.

More grammar, first. As you remember, a noun is a word that means a thing or person; a noun phrase is a string of words that can be used wherever a noun can be used, and might simply be a noun on its own. So, imagine this:

> **The grey alien** loves **the pink plastic spade**.

Here *the grey alien* and *the pink plastic spade* are both noun phrases. You can tell because you can drop simple nouns in and it makes sense: *Mike loves Steve.*

So, a noun phrase fragment means a fragment which is just a noun phrase, not a full sentence. Confused? Don't be, it's easy when you see an example.

> I stumbled off the bus, oblivious to the screams around me. A wail filled my ears, deep and loud: it made the buildings shake and my stomach tremble. Because, there it was, towering over the stadium.
> **The massive baby.**

Yes, *the massive baby* is a fragment. There's no verb. The massive baby what? A noun phrase is not a sentence, not by any definition of grammar. That means, if you're using noun phrases as fragments, and you're not in anything that can claim to be speech, you're definitely breaking the rules.

I think it's icky. Your mind expects the noun phrase to be followed by a verb and it's not, and you just sort of catch your finger on the end of the sentence and draw a tiny bit of blood. I don't need the disjointed feel that fragments give me here, so why bother? Having said that, enough people do this that it seems to be a thing.

Fortunately, there is a very simple fix.

> There it was, towering over the stadium: the massive baby.

Yes, I know. It feels like you've softened the punchline because you haven't thundered that full stop down. But, c'mon. Grammar exists for a reason. You have to choose between your reader's comfort and your desire for drama.

Lights, camera, fragments

I put this in front of a bunch of readers, who were also writers. It generated a lot of discussion! They said that they used fragments more than I did, and that I shouldn't just write off a style because I didn't like it. Although to be clear, no one is claiming you should write a novel using only incomplete sentences, come now, we are not postmodernists.

Now, you should do this, too. Not be a postmodernist, obviously. No, you should seek healthy criticism on your work, because it's something which will make you better! I've learnt from more people than I can count who've told me what I was doing wrong. So, I understand why they feel that this is a thing. And, frankly, this goes for a lot of the rest of this book, too.

The one thing which I will say, though, is this.

Editors and agents are looking at this stuff. Yes, you can point to books on the shelf of your local bookshop which contain fragments. But you're not published, so you shouldn't use them as examples of what is permissible. No, I agree that it's not fair; but we need to play a different, harder game to those authors. If you're going to break these rules and use fragments, you need to do it very, very judiciously. And by very, very judiciously, I mean, close to never.

Probably the one place where the rules are a bit more permeable is that fragments give you a splintered feel which can move the narrative forward. As a fragment hater, I found it hard to write an action sequence with fragments that felt acceptable. But for you, just you, I tried.

> Eric rolled aside. The blade splintered the floor where his shoulder had been. Bonetongue grimaced and tugged it free, showering him with wood chippings.
>
> Eric scrambled backwards. **Heart pounding.**
>
> I'm not going to die here, he thought. **If I can just...**
>
> His feet slipped in blood.
>
> The demon grinned and lifted its knife again. It licked its face, pale head gleaming in the dim light. It hissed. Then, it lunged.
>
> It was fast, but this time Eric was ready. Instead of dodging back, he hurled himself forwards, between its legs; the cleaver blade whispered past him and sank into the floorboards with a thud. He grabbed his gun, lying on the floor behind it. With the demon struggling with its weapon, he aimed and fired.
>
> **One, two, three.** The shots were as loud as thunderbolts in the tiny room. It staggered, keening and hissing. Then it turned, roared, and leapt at him, its pallid spindly arms outstretched.

Three fragments.

The first, *heart pounding,* is a really nasty one. I'm dropping the word *his* to make the fragment. But this, I think, is the classic action fragment. What does it get me? Well, I definitely lose one word, and in this case, yeah, it's not going great for Eric, so maybe the sharp nature of fragments is appropriate. But I've broken the rules, made the text that bit harder to read, and all I got was one less measly word. Is it worth it?

My opinion is no, it's not.

If I can just... This is reported thought, and therefore doesn't break the rules. However, *if I can just...* style fragments are clichés, but at least I tried to indicate what caused him to lose concentration. I dislike it. You could actually delete it and the passage would lose nothing.

The third is more interesting. *One, two, three* is a true rule-breaking fragment. I used it at the fulcrum of the piece, where the action is at peak and the tables are turned.

The reason I could be able to get away with this one is that it might be reported thought. Or it might be not. I've intentionally muddied the narrator's voice with the character's voice. Perhaps Eric is counting bullets under his breath. It's like when we have a countdown in the narrative, and the narrator drops in little fragments *like fifteen seconds until it blows*. Maybe that's the narrator telling us, maybe it's the protagonist checking their watch, and we're going so fast that it's not important to know. However, this is a really irritating technique if overused, and I'm in the camp of any use at all being overuse.

But look, you could defragment it and actually the whole thing would still work.

> He fired three times. The shots were as loud as thunderbolts in the tiny room.

See? Worth risking an editor's or agent's ire for that?

Summary

Fragments are incomplete sentences: that means they are missing things. Sentences like *yes*, *ouch*, or *whoops* aren't fragments, they are interjections. However, interjections suffer from some of the same consequences as fragments, so treat them in a similar way.

Fragments make your text jagged and splintered, and tax your reader. We use them in speech, sometimes. Even though people in real life talk in fragments all the time, in fiction only use them to indicate, e.g. distraction or being prevented from talking. Be wary of overuse and cliched use. However, occasional fragments can be used to good effect.

Use them also in inner thoughts, with the same caveats.

Noun fragments are fragments with no verb. For example:

    The charging elephant.

These are almost always wrong. It's tempting to use them as punchlines: don't. Use a colon to link them to the previous sentence.

Fragments in action are complicated, especially when you're muddying the narrative voice. Throwing them around with abandon will be irritating.

Further reading

Here's a piece from an editor who is a little more pro-fragments than I am. She makes some excellent points. https://wintersediting.com/sentence-fragments/ I just realised one of her examples is about a Colin, too, which is a coincidence – I named my Colin after the old friend I'd just gone for a drink with. Maybe this is is now part of an extended Colinverse. I did, however, totally steal her idea to use that *Hunger Games* bit, although I ended up writing my own.

And here's another piece from a different writer who is much more pro-fragments. It lays out the argument as to why they might be okay. It's worth reading for balance, maybe? https://www.darcypattison.com/writing/revision/sentence-fragments-use-for-conversational-tone/

Then, this is a piece on fragments from an editor who is, I think, rather more realistic about them, and makes it very clear how unfair the whole thing is. https://www.novelpublicity.com/2012/03/ask-the-editor-is-it-okay-to-use-sentence-fragments-in-my-writing-how-much-is-too-much/

Lastly, the Wikipedia page on interjections is fascinating, if you're as much of a grammar nerd as I am. https://en.wikipedia.org/wiki/Interjection

Chapter 5

I held it and realised its pronoun was ambiguous

Lucas likes pronouns

Pronouns are a part of grammar that are having their day in the sun at the moment. That's good: knowing what a pronoun is will help you get your teeth into this section. Here I'm going to talk about a common error with pronouns, one that almost always provokes unintentional mirth from your reader. And we don't want that, now, do we?

First, let's remind ourselves how they actually work. Make of this what you will:

> Lucas sat in the chair. Lucas liked the chair. Lucas wanted to look out the window, so that Lucas could see the subjects that Lucas ruled with an iron fist. Lucas was happy.

There are no pronouns there, and it feels very childlike. We imagine that this might be a caveman or the Hulk or

Animal from the Muppets: in other words, dropping pronouns is a cliched shorthand for someone primitive.

Perhaps that's a trope because our minds do an unbelievable amount of work when we read, and pronoun substitution is definitely one of the more complicated jobs. Thanks to the amazing machinery in your skull, we can rewrite the previous example, and it will still be comprehensible, like this.

> Lucas sat in the chair. **He** liked **it**. **He** wanted to look out the window, so that **he** could see the subjects that **he** ruled with an iron fist. Lucas was happy.

I kept the last *Lucas* for comic effect; it maintains the childishness of it.

Notice how you know exactly which noun a particular pronoun refers to. The gender and grammatical number of the pronoun helps you here. You know what gender means; grammatical number is the fancy phrase that says whether a word is singular or plural. They both have to be the same as the gender and grammatical number of the noun that the pronoun refers to.

So, we didn't refer to the chair or window as *he*, because chairs don't conventionally have a gender; we didn't call Lucas's ruled subjects *it* or *he* because subjects are plural and *it* and *he* are singular. However, there's still a lot of potential ambiguity here. Your job, when you're line editing, is to make sure there's none.

It is ambiguous

Try this.

> He picked up the cake and held it up to the light. **It** was small and heavy, and would surely feed the vampires.

You can see what the problem here is, right? That's right: the second *it*, the one I bolded, is ambiguous. Fascinatingly, you actually know what it refers to, for two reasons: I've reinforced the use of *it* as the cake, so your brain sorta goes with it, and obviously because draculas don't eat lights. But it's still the kind of thing that the haters can scoff about; and, more importantly, you're piling more work onto your reader.

These can be quite hard to correct. In this case, the light doesn't really bring anything to the table, so I'm just going to ditch it.

> He picked up the cake. It was small and heavy, and would surely feed the vampires.

Here's a more complicated one.

> The rain drenched Lucas. **It** drove down like darts, hard and cold, and rattled off the cobbles. He squinted through **it**, towards the prison gatehouse. **It** was lit up like the entrance to hell, by a single smoking torch. **Its** guttering red

flame painted the stone walls in crimson and shadow.

Lucas shivered at the sight of **it**, and clutched the cake bag closer to himself.

So, here's your question. What is Lucas actually shivering at the sight of?

I intended him to be spooked by the prison gatehouse. But I've used *it* so much that I've muddied the waters, and it could be that you think he's unnerved by the torch: if so, that will confuse you, because you'll think that the torch is important rather than just being a bit of descriptive flavour, and I'll end up with Chekhov's unused torch.

Well, we've done half the struggle: we've identified that there's an ambiguous pronoun. Well done. So how do we fix it?

It seems like I write 'you have two solutions' every other page, but here we are again. You have two... No, I'm all self-conscious now.

Solution one: substitute the pronoun for a noun.

> Lucas shivered at the sight of **those metal doors**, and clutched the cake bag to himself.

This is longer, but completely unambiguous. I couldn't write *the prison gatehouse* because that would echo (we'll look at that in chapter thirteen) so I used a synonym. This is quite a nice fix.

However, the reality is, it's not enough. I also massively overused the word *it* in the previous paragraph which is why

I got myself into this mess. So, if I go there and prune them back, it will also fix my ambiguity, because I can remove the one critical *it* which gets me into this trouble. So, solution two is to make sure there are no other nouns in between our pronoun and the noun it's supposed to refer to.

> The rain drove down like darts, hard and cold. **It** rattled off the cobbles, and **it** hammered down on Lucas as he strode to the prison gatehouse, making him squint and curse.
>
> The stone building was lit up like the entrance to hell. A single smoking torch painted the walls crimson, and the shadows writhed from the guttering flame.
>
> Lucas knew what was within that grim building, and shivered at the sight of **it**. He clutched the cake bag closer to himself.

My previous use of *squinted* was actually filtering, so I cleaned that up while I was there. What I've done is found a way to put a noun so that it's the closest noun to the pronoun. That had the effect of changing the rhythm of the rest of it, and so I pruned the *its* because the sheer quantity of them made it a bit wooden, and that meant some of the sentences got split and some got joined together. It's not fantastic, still: *knew* feels a little filtery, so maybe I could do another pass. However, my pronouns are unambiguous, and that's enough for now.

It's good to note that you don't just get this with *it*: all the pronouns have this problem. However, I find that I do it mostly with *it*, probably because the number of props outnumbers the number of characters.

They're important to think about

Here's another problem.

> Lucas threw the cake down into the head vampire's cage. **They** picked it up, and sunk **their** fangs into it. Lucas's guards shifted uneasily behind him. He was ready to attack **them** if need be.

Here the tyrant Lucas is feeding a vampire. But, my vampire is using *they* as a pronoun. And we are now in ambiguity city, population, us. Who is Lucas ready to attack?

The problem with *them* and *they* is that its grammatical number can be either one (for singular non-binary people) or many (for a group of people or things). So we get a bit of confusion between Lucas's guards and the cake eating night-walker.

This is really, really hard. The general consensus seems to be to use proper nouns to resolve this. So, in times when it's unclear, keep *they* for groups, and use names for individuals. In which case, we'd write this.

> Lucas threw the cake down into the head vampire's cage. **They** picked it up, and sunk **their** fangs into it. Lucas's guards shifted

uneasily behind him. He was ready to attack
Andra if need be.

The *they* and *there* I left are unambiguous, because the
guards aren't mentioned. As soon as they are, *them* is now
ambiguous, so I clear it up by using their name, instead.

This isn't as bad as it sounds. After all, we use a lot of
proper nouns when we have two or more people of the same
gender in a scene, because then we have ambiguity over *he*
and *she*. But you're going to see more with *they*, and that's
fine.

Some authors use other, more alien, pronouns instead of
they, like *xe*. Becky Chambers does this all the time. These
are easier to disambiguate and therefore easier to read, but
aren't what people say today, and definitely have a 'space'
feel. That probably means they're only good for spec fic,
which is a pity, because they're much easier to understand.

The reality is if you have non-binary characters, you are
going to have to go through your *them* and *they* pronouns and
be sure that they are unambiguous. If that means using
nouns more often, so be it.

They's a crowd

This is, if I'm going to be honest, a pet peeve and not really
anything to do with pronouns.

> The crowd muttered the names of vegetables
> and shook their fists at the stage. **They** growled
> angrily when Lucas appeared: **they** wanted

blood, and the death of the hated vampires. The tyrant Lucas would do that for them.

They muttered some more vegetable names.

The whole crowd muttered and growled? No, of course they didn't. Some people at the front probably did. The ones who turned up for the free vampire cake are at the back talking about shoe prices and ignoring the whole thing. If you find yourself using *they* a lot, ask yourself, is it because I'm writing crowds as homogenous masses of identical people? If so, that's not very good. You're generally better off focussing on individuals rather than on a group.

Summary

He, *she*, *they* and *it* are examples of pronouns. The main danger with pronouns is ambiguity, where it's not clear what noun that the pronoun refers to.

> The girl picked up her kite and her dog, and then threw **it** off the cliff.

To solve, you can substitute the pronoun for a noun, or you can move a noun to be closer to the pronoun.

> The girl picked up **her kite** and her dog, and threw **the kite** off the cliff.

   The girl picked up her dog and **her kite**, and threw **it** off the cliff.

They is particularly hard, because it can refer to a group or a non-binary individual. If you end up with ambiguity, keep the *they* for groups, and use the individual's name instead of a pronoun.

If you're using *they* too much, is it because you've written a crowd as a mass of people? Look at individuals.

Chapter 6

I carefully stopped using adverbs

Meet hungry Mr King

If you've been in the writing game for any period of time, you'll have heard that piece of advice about adverbs. Never use them, they'll mutter. Stephen King said so, they'll murmur. They're bad, they'll whisper. Bad, bad, bad...

And when you round on them, screaming, why? They'll slink away, shaking their heads. And you'll be left standing with nothing but a feather boa and a half-eaten tub of cream cheese. Which I mean, hey, that's all you need for a good night in right there.

So let's figure out what's going on here.

Before we get in too deep, let's remind ourselves what adverbs actually are. An adverb is a word that modifies a non-noun, by describing it. We're actually going to only talk about the adverbs that modify verbs in this chapter; adverbs that modify adjectives can get a shout out in the adjective chapter because really they're just compound adjectives. As always, it's easier to show than tell, so I'll do that, and I'll also use this chapter to workshop my Stephen King fanfic with you. Let's start with this.

> Stephen King sat down **heavily** in the chair. His mechanical legs twitched **suddenly**, and his cat **quickly** moved from under him. 'I'm sorry, Clovis,' he hissed, **dangerously**. 'There's a zombie in the building.'

Oh, in my fanfic Stephen King is the CEO of the Happy Pencil Corp by day, and a vampire robot that hunts zombies by night. Pretty cool, right?

The classic advice about identifying adverbs is that they end in *ly*. This is wrong, but as we'll see, for practical purposes it's quite useful. However, my superior way of deciding if something is an adverb is to ask, will Stephen King eat it? If he does, then it's an adverb. If he doesn't, it's not! This doesn't catch them all, but it's good, as you'll see.

Let's apply the rule, and the hungry Mr King will get to work for us. In my fanfic above, there are four words that end in *ly*, and Stephen King will eat it *heavily*, *suddenly*, *quickly* and *dangerously*.

So, yes, those are all adverbs. Sometimes it might work but sound a bit weird; in this case, try putting the potential adverb before the *eat it*. For example, *Stephen King will definitely eat it* shows that *definitely* is also an adverb.

We now have an excellent adverb detector, which means we can root them out wherever they hide. So what is it that people hate about adverbs?

48

It's that maddening thing, 'show, don't tell.' When you use an adverb, you're telling us what's happening. You're not immersing us in the world: you're not making it real by showing us the action and the consequences of the action. Now, most writing guides stop at this point. Don't use adverbs, they say! If you read such a guide, a fun thing to do is to see how many adverbs the writer has written up to this point. And you can do that by understanding that the rule of adverbs ending in *ly* is, well, it's not very good.

For example, did you know that *inside* is an adverb? It's a so-called adverb of place. *His space axe glittered inside the King-mobile.* The verb is *glittered*, and everything after the verb is part of an adverbial phrase, a fragment which is acting as an adverb. And to test it: will Stephen King eat it? Yes. *Stephen King will eat it inside the King-mobile.*

Adverbs of time are even crazier. *Tomorrow, before,* and *then* are adverbs. *Then!* *Stephen King will eat it then.* Yep. Checks out.

So if we banish adverbs completely, we make it very difficult to describe the relationships between things in time and space. Yes, show don't tell, but also, sometimes, tell us that the zombie is on the car (*Stephen King will eat it on the car*), otherwise what the heck is happening when the green hands smash through the sunroof? (*Stephen King will eat it through the sunroof.*)

All this is a long way of demonstrating that the rules governing adverbs are more complicated and nuanced than just saying 'don't use them.' As a result, In this chapter I've tried to give you guidance on times to definitely not use them, and why, and how to fix it; and then to talk about times when adverbs are fine, but that then still leaves a huge grey zone in between where you (yes, you) need to use your skill and judgement to decide what to do with them.

My verbs are weak, I cannot see, I used adverbs like beautifully

Let's start with the easiest, which is when an adverb is propping up a weak verb.

> The zombie moved **quickly** away from Stephen King.

Quickly (and its relatives which describe other speeds of actions) are usually a hint that you're using a weak verb. These adverbs often end in a *ly*, which is why that rule works, by the way. And the first rule of adverb hunting is to ask yourself, can I make the verb stronger and delete the adverb?

> The zombie **scurried** away from Stephen King.

Moved is a really weak verb, so I beefed it up by transforming it into *scurried*, and lost a word, too. A fair number of your adverbs will probably be culled by this first step, and your prose will be leaner as a result.

Great, step two. Redundant and subjective adverbs.

> Stephen King sprinted **quickly** after it.

Here, *sprinted* is a nice strong verb. You can imagine the pistons pumping on his undead legs, as he hurtles through the corridors of the Happy Pencil Corp HQ. The adverb isn't propping anything up. Can it stay?

No, because it's redundant. You always sprint quickly, and so it's not bringing anything to the party. The easiest thing is to just delete them. Yes, the temptation is there to reinforce the verb; if that's the case, ask yourself: am I back to propping up the verb? Is there a stronger one than sprinted? Maybe not, in which case, let's take it out and move the action along more quickly.

Subjective adverbs are dealt with the same way. These are adverbs which are right at the end of the 'tell' spectrum; things like beautifully. This is a subjective opinion of the author, not shown by the text. Generally, you'll delete these without a second thought. We're not going to look at this too closely here, because we'll cover redundancy and subjectivity in adjectives, later in chapter nine, as the same rules apply to them.

He said angrily

Now, the one that Mr King hates the most is adverbs on speech tags.

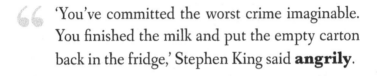

'You've committed the worst crime imaginable. You finished the milk and put the empty carton back in the fridge,' Stephen King said **angrily**.

Yeah, we're gonna see some Stephen King vigilante action now! But wait, I hear you say, perhaps angrily. What

51

about the adverb on the speech tag? *Angrily* is an adverb, right?

Why, yes, it is. I'm telling you that he's angry. But I'm not, if we're going to be honest with ourselves, showing it. If you read the line without the tag, he just sounds a bit miffed. So I'm telling, and what I'm telling isn't really lining up with what I'm showing. It's not redundant, although it's perhaps a tiny bit subjective. Well, let's try the first rule, and beef up the verb.

> 'You've committed the worst crime imaginable. You finished the milk and put the empty carton back in the fridge,' Stephen King **screamed**.

My text is now a little terser, and my verb, *screamed*, is doing some great work. But let's be honest, the actual speech is still really weak. We're not getting rage, really. Just sort of zombie-milk-induced apathy. So, for adverbs on speech tags, we have another and better option, which is to just rewrite the speech so that the adverb is unnecessary. We're going to move from tell to show.

> 'You disgust me! You've betrayed them, all of them! They opened the fridge, expecting to find milk, and they... found... nothing!' Stephen King **screamed**.

I pumped the anger up to eleven. Now you can see the veins in his robot neck really standing out, can't you? The *screamed* is almost redundant; it's pretty obvious that his fanged mouth is wide open, and spittle is flying everywhere. If there was context as to who was speaking, we could definitely omit the speech tag completely. Here's a great place to put an action beat in (more on them later, in chapter fourteen).

> 'You disgust me!' Stephen King's huge metal fingers folded around the zombie. 'You have betrayed them, all of them! They opened the fridge, expecting to find milk, and they... found... nothing!'

This is better because using too many strong verbs as speech tags is generally considered bad form. We'll talk about this in the speech tag chapter, chapter fourteen. But the lesson here is that the adverb on the speech tag showed us that we might need stronger speech; the adverb wasn't propping up a weak verb, it was propping up weak speech.

Suddenly I wasn't sure

Next: immediacy. For this, the cure is unpleasant. You may well end up rewriting the sentence. This is because these adverbs are ones which don't have either verbs or speech which can be propped up, and will change the sense of the sentence if deleted. Immediacy adverbs are adverbs which are showing how things happened in time.

An example:

> **Suddenly**, a hundred zombies ran into the room.

Oh no! The tables have turned on Stephen King!

Suddenly is always a red flag: here we are absolutely telling rather than showing. We're asking the reader to accept that, you know, this just happened, without explaining why. It's a subjective adverb, too. Who is it sudden for?

It's hard to fix, though. There's no verb which means *suddenly ran*, so we can't use option one: replace the adverb-verb pair with a stronger verb. It's not a speech tag so there's no speech for us to rewrite for option three. If we tried option two, deletion, it changes the sense of the sentence.

> A hundred zombies ran into the room.

It's lost something, hasn't it? The immediacy has gone. Okay, how can we put the urgency back, but without an adverb? I think the reality is, we need a rewrite. I'm going to try and put the feeling of *suddenly* in without saying it.

> With a roar like an enraged squirrel, a hundred zombies **crashed** through the wall, showering Stephen King with brick dust.

Crashed implies immediacy. I didn't want the zombies to crash into the room because that means something else, so through the wall they went. I chucked in all the rest to really hammer home how fast they were going. Here, I'm doing my best to immerse you in the world using strong verbs and the consequences of those strong verbs. And I think it reads better, right?

This is one fix, but it's actually not the best one. With

suddenly, you should take a look at the broader text. There are a few dangers that this pernicious little word is surfacing.

You might want to write *suddenly* because you're emulating a jump scare from a movie. Well, books don't have jump scares, so this is going to need a rethink. Books can still have sudden, shocking events, which leave you reeling: but the unexpectedness comes from story, not the words. My favourite is the 'red wedding' chapter in *A Storm of Swords* by George R R Martin, which does actually have a single *suddenly* in it, although that's a throw-away one, and the text doesn't really need it. The horror of this passage comes from the way that all these familiar characters are brutally cut down.

The other problem that *suddenly* could be showing is a bit of small-scale *deus ex machina*. The zombie is coming for Stephen King but he suddenly finds a mechanical punching fist in the King-mobile. This is unsatisfying, and the use of *suddenly* is trying to hide that. This will need a structural rework: you're going to need to ramp up the tension and the solution to make this episode enjoyable to read.

Scarily we're not quite done

Let's just finish with a quick round up of some other adverb shenanigans.

Hedging is when you use adverbs to hedge your bets around what is happening in the world. *Probably, actually* and *basically* are the ones to look out for here, although there are others too. We'll talk about these later on what I call 'descriptive certainty' which demands its own whole chapter, chapter fifteen. Lastly, (yes, that's an adverb) *obviously* is a special weasel word, worse even than *suddenly*, and we'll talk about that in chapter twelve.

Exhausted yet? Remember, the rules are simple. For the classes of adverbs above, they are all indications that you have a weakness somewhere: to fix them, you can improve your verb, improve your speech, improve your text, or simply delete the adverb. Playing around with different versions of a sentence will produce results that work in one place but not another, and so it's worth tinkering a bit.

When you're messing with sentence structure, some people say that reading aloud is a good thing to try. It's never worked for me, but I'm one of those people with an over-whelmingly loud inner voice, so I don't get much from that, plus I feel self-conscious talking to myself on public transport.

Incredibly we might summarize with adverbs

We've talked a lot about the times when you should remove adverbs. However, I think there are some cases when you can get away with adverbs. The first is when you are summarising.

Summarising is when you move the plot along, and there is information that your reader needs to understand the context, but you don't want to dwell on it because it's either boring or distracting. When you summarise, you tell, you don't show.

When I mentioned the red wedding above, I said that the characters were brutally cut down. *Brutally* is an adverb, and I could remove it: but I have no interest in going into detail about this harrowing chapter, and so I summarised, and left that adverb to give a tiny bit of flavour. Adverbs are a very terse way of putting sparkle into summary.

Choosing the correct amount of summary is a key art of storytelling. If you summarise too much, your reader will have no emotional investment and the thing will read like a Wikipedia entry. If there's too little, you'll grind out endless details and your reader will again have no emotional investment, because they'll have given up.

You need to ask yourself: do I need this at all? If I'm summarising, say, travel to Egypt, should I just delete it, and cut to Stephen King landing in front of the Great Pyramid of Giza, the sand boiling around him, the camels delighted, the tourists screaming with glee? We care about the musicality of the prose, summary is boring and leaden, so I might not want it... But also maybe I have pages of him flying over the Atlantic which is dull as heck, and needs reducing to a few paragraphs.

So if you decide that, yes, a bit of summary is needed, then maybe adverbs will give that summary some flavour. In that case, though, make those adverbs work! Have a long line of them outside, hope in their eyes, desperate to make the cut. Choose only the strongest.

This means don't break the above rules, even in your summarising; just don't feel as guilty when you drop your adverbs in.

Equally clever

When the adverb is actually the important bit of information in the sentence, it stays.

The cake wasn't divided **equally** between the zombies.

The word *equally* is the cornerstone here. Deleting it doesn't just change the timbre of the sentence, it changes the entire meaning. You could rewrite it to say something about how the zombies got different sized slices, but why bother? This is punchy and simple. Oh, and the zombie that got the smallest cake slice? He's the one who put the empty milk carton in the fridge. Justice is served.

With speech tags, keeping adverbs might be excused if you really have no way of indicating that through the speech. This might be subtle inflections to volume or tone of the speaker. *Sarcastically* and *quietly* are good examples: speaking quietly is not whispering, and if it really matters that you say that, well, then there's no other verb, and of course the point of sarcasm is that you can't tell from the text. But really think about whether it's worth it. Adverbs on speech tags will bog down the flow. As an aside, I dislike sarcasm because I think the sarcastic hero is a massively overused and underfunny trope, so I avoid that.

However, you have one gold-plated reason to use adverbs. That's when the adverb is startling. Its inclusion is adding art to the sentence.

 Stephen King staggered **solemnly**.

This is weird, because staggering has very little to do with solemnity. The juxtaposition of the verb and the adverb is startling, and therefore good. In this case Mr King has had a little too much cake, but he needs to make a moving speech to his new zombie friends.

Yes, like all the best fanfic, it has ended happily.

Summary

In this chapter we looked at adverbs. Keep an eye out for *ly*, although remember hungry Mr King. You will ask yourself:

Is the adverb propping up a weak verb? E.g. *moved quickly*. If so, improve the verb.

Is the adverb redundant? E.g. *ran quickly*. If so, delete it.

Is the adverb subjective? E.g. *jumped beautifully*. If so, delete it.

Is the adverb propping up weak direct speech? E.g. *said angrily*. If so, improve the speech.

Is the adverb propping up a weak sense of immediacy? E.g. *suddenly*. If so, rewrite.

Is the adverb hedging? E.g. *probably*. If so, rewrite.

Is the adverb the key of the sentence? If so, keep.

Is the adverb for making summary terse? If so, re-evaluate your use of summary, and maybe, keep, maybe, either delete the summary or fill it out.

Is the adverb startling and well written? If so, keep it, and laugh at your foolish enemies.

Otherwise... think hard about what you're writing. Is the adverb making your prose better, or hiding another flaw that we've not covered?

Further reading

First, here's what Stephen King actually says. I'm not sure what he will think if he ever reads my fanfic, so let's not tell him, eh? https://www.themarginalian.org/2013/03/13/stephen-king-on-adverbs/

Louise Harnby is reliably good. Here she's much more positive and nuanced than Mr King. https://www.louiseharnbyproofreader.com/blog/using-adverbs-in-fiction-writing-clunk-versus-clarity

This blog says the usual stuff, but makes a case that adverbs can be good in blurbs because they are great for summarisation. I am terrible at blurbs and therefore have no useful opinion. https://www.ignitedinkwriting.com/ignite-your-ink-blog-for-writers/why-creative-writers-shouldnt-use-adverbs-most-of-the-time/2019

Lastly, you can read the red wedding here. It probably goes without saying (yet, I will say it anyway) that it is very, very bloody. https://www.today.com/popculture/red-wedding-read-infamous-chapter-george-r-r-martins-game-6c10208389 If you read it, look at how GRRM uses adverbs. He's pretty light with them, and even then you could argue that you could get rid of a fair few of the ones he uses and the chapter would lose nothing.

Chapter 7

It is time to use contractions

It's going to be fine

Adverbs were big and scary, and I'm sure adjectives will be too; so let's take a quick breather, and do an easy, short one. In this chapter we're going to look at contractions.

What's a contraction? Well, I just used one, then! They're when you take two words, and you squidge them together into a single word. They tend to have apostrophes in them, because letters get broken off and dropped on the floor when the words are smooshed into each other, and we use apostrophes to indicate what's missing. Your favourite and mine is the word *it's*. This is, of course, a short form of *it is* and the *i* got replaced with an apostrophe when the two words were glued together. (And, as we also all know, *it's* never ever means *the thing that belongs to it*, because English is awful.)

The line edit technique this time is easy: give yourself

permissions to use contractions. Although, as always, I'll talk about when it's cool not to, and not cool to.

First, though, why do we want to use them at all?

Contractions are a natural evolution of the language and have been around for as long as English has. Yes, the Victorian middle classes were horrified by them, but that was an isolated fad. Shakespeare, writing hundreds of years before, uses them all over the place: although, fascinatingly, Elizabethan contractions are different to modern contractions, and it's one of the things that makes old Bill Shakespeare so hard to read today.

 For his bounty,
There was no winter **in't**; an autumn **'twas**
That grew the more by reaping. His delights
Were dolphin-like: they show'd his back above
The element they liv'd in.

This is from *Anthony and Cleopatra*. Some of these are actually elisions, not contractions, where letters are lost from words: *show'd* and *liv'd* are examples of this and are there to make the rhythm work. However *in't* is an old way of contracting *in it*, and *'twas* is *it was*.

Contractions don't just move us forward or backwards in time: they also move us around the world: *y'all* from the US, *g'wan* from the Caribbean, for example, and that's because the way that they are constructed tends to come from the accent of the speaker. We all use them, endlessly, and we're so used to them that we barely notice them.

They're such a part of the fabric of the language that they're a great way to shorten your text.

You have, I hope, noticed a theme through this book. Keep it punchy. Keep it quick. Hone every sentence so it's as sharp and balanced as a knife. So, if you can find a way to make your text easier to read, with no cost to meaning or structure, you take it. Contractions are your friend.

This is obvious, right? Why am I saying this?

Well, for one, I've seen the latest version of Microsoft Word telling me not to use them, because they sound informal. I think that Word is rather geared to writing documents about load-bearing tangents, rather than people hanging off bridges, gasping for help: so, yeah Word, go point your paper clip elsewhere.

But also, I always forget to contract! I think it's because I cut stuff up in the edit process, and then forget to put it back together. I had to scan back loads when I wrote this, and close some *it is* into *it's*, a *they are* into a *they're*, and I'm still sure I missed some (in fact I literally just corrected that *I'm*).

So, as long as you're being purposeful about your contractions, they're a cheap way of sharpening your prose.

Do not mindlessly contract

So, contractions aren't always good, are they?

No. No, they are not.

> 'I **will not** get onto that jet-ski.' Janet's nose wrinkled. 'It **has not** been cleaned for weeks.'

Two candidates for contracting here: *will not* and *has not*. I'd contract the second to *hasn't* and leave the first. Why? Because the emphasis is on the *not* in Janet's first sentence. You could even imagine italicising that *not*, to show her huge disdain for the dirty jet-ski (and we'll speak about that later). I personally wouldn't do that because that's not how I write, but keeping it uncontracted lets her dislike jump out.

So here, we're exploiting the fact that when people contract, it's due to them speaking casually. When you remove the contractions, you introduce formality: it sounds like Janet's being fussy. This can be a nice little tool: it's very subtle.

You also have to be careful with idiomatic contractions. *Ain't* is a great example of this: it's not a universally used contraction like, say, *we'll*, and so you're using a particular voice in your narrative, and you need to decide if that voice is welcome to your reader.

This, like all the things we've covered, is a choice, not a rule. For example, it could work amazingly if you decide to use idiomatic Victorian contractions, like *shan't* (*shall not*), *mayn't* (*may not*), or *warn't* (*were not*). You'll make your speaker's or narrator's voice really pop... But the price will be your reader's ease of comprehension. As a result, most writers stay in more idiomatic contractions, and live with the fact that they're not faithfully reproducing the accent they're writing in.

Compare and contrast these.

'**Thou'st** prepared, sire? **'Tis** nearly **morn.**'

'**Are you** ready, sir? It's nearly **morning.**'

Yes, I cheated slightly, I changed some words, because no one says *are you prepared?* But the fact is, one is a cod-medieval utterance, and you can practically smell the mud and the feudal system; the other is much more modern. Using modern contractions in a historical or fantasy setting grounds it, and makes it more earthy, and is an easy trick if that's what you're after. Against that, your readers might have an expectation of full-blown *thine* and *thee*, or maybe you're so authentic that you're going to reproduce historical speech and it will look out of place surrounded by modern contractions. Point is, think about it, balance the load you're laying on your reader with the authenticity.

Lastly, while we're in the realm of science fiction and fantasy, here's a thing that seems to crop up only there.

Omitting contractions makes speech sound pompous, and so I think it became a cliché in seventies spec fic to have powerful non-humans speak in full words; and we somehow all inherited this trope without realising it. So, aliens, angels and elves all seem to drop contractions. (There's even a throwaway joke about that on *The Orville*, so I'm not the only person to notice that.)

Again, I think if you do it, do it consciously. Embrace it and go all in, or don't do it at all. I personally think it's a cliché, but I've seen it in very recently published books by successful novelists. So when they have an eleven headed alien angel say 'it is now the time that we have foreseen, we are sure that it is nearing the end,' or some such, well, maybe that's a thing that they can get away with because they've already sold a billion copies of earlier books.

Summary

Contract away! It's not bad writing. However, do it consciously. In particular, be aware that contractions carry a voice, and that voice can be tiring to read. However, omitting them can be just as exhausting, because it sounds pompous.

Further reading

This is my favourite thing on the entire internet about contractions. https://quillpenandblotter.wordpress.com/2017/07/23/contractions-are-historical-yall/comment-page-1/

Chapter 8

The passive voice was used by me

Being passive

Look, I'm procrastinating about the adjectives chapter. Can you blame me? But that's not why I wrote this one now.

I got dinged by a critique partner recently for use of the passive voice, with good reason. Why? Because I'd never really sat down and studied it. So, in an effort to make my writing better, I thought I'd do this one now and adjectives can wait. And you can suffer along with me.

You might have forgotten, so here's a quick refresher: nouns (*shark, octopus*) are used by verbs (*yodelled, laughed*). The noun which does the verb is the called the 'subject.' (***The octopus*** *laughed.*) The noun on the receiving end of the verb is the 'object'. (*The octopus laughed at **the shark.***) In English the normal order is subject, then verb, then object. So, for example, *the shark ignored the octopus* is in this order. The shark is doing the ignoring, and so is the subject; then comes the verb; then the object is the octopus which is being ignored. I'd make a joke about the octopus at this point, but I think we all agree that would just encourage her.

However, there is a second order that's used in English, and that's object, verb, subject. When you write this way, it's called the passive voice.

You know the drill by now; let's show an example.

> **The gun** was **picked** up by **Janet** with moments to spare.

The verb is *picked*. The subject is *Janet*: she's the one doing the picking up. The object is *the gun*. That's the thing being picked up. The rest is a great big adverbial phrase (*Steven King will eat it with moments to spare*) and I put that in because for whatever reason they hide the passive voice from me. If you strip that out, it's really easy to see how clunky it looks:

> **The gun** was **picked** up by **Janet**.

So object, verb, subject.

There's a magic little word in passive sentences: that's *was*. It's needed to make the grammar work. Here's another example.

> **Janet was sent** sprawling by a vicious left hook from **von Klicken**.

So, the verb is *sent*. The subject is *von Klicken*, and the object is *Janet*. And note that Janet, the subject, is right at the start of the sentence. Subject, verb, object. And there's that little old *was* again.

(Now, a small aside for the pedants. The passive voice is not *actually* object-verb-subject. If you wish, you can go and try and untangle the Wikipedia entry to see why not: I'll drop it in the further reading section for you. But, honestly, thinking about it this way is so much easier to reason about.)

Being too passive

So what's the problem with passive voice?

There are two complaints: the first is that it makes your writing more, well, passive. The passive voice sounds detached, removed from the action and its consequences. This is, of course, why it's used by human resources departments the world over. 'It was decided that...' is how you're going to be told that there's no more company-provided tap dancing sessions.

The second is more mechanical. Make it go faster, lose the redundant words, keep it rolling at breakneck pace: that's our motto. Every word we don't need is a word that stands between us and our incredibly attractive and intelligent readers. (Who, by the way, are looking very good today. Did they do something new with their hair?)

Let's go back to our first example.

66 The gun **was** picked up by Janet with moments to spare.

The solution, in this case, is very easy. Restructure the

sentence so that the subject is first. With a bit of luck, you'll end up with a shorter sentence; and we'll talk about why you might not later.

> Janet picked up by the gun with moments to spare.

This is just nicer. It's sharper and simpler. Note the lack of *was*: that's an easy tell to show that we're not passive any more. What about the other one?

> Janet **was** sent sprawling by a vicious left hook from von Klicken.

How about this:

> A vicious left hook from von Klicken sent Janet sprawling.

Or even:

> Von Klicken's vicious left hook sent Janet sprawling.

In this case, it does read better. It's more immediate, and we deleted words yet retained the same meaning. Get up, Janet: only you can save the world...

So, that's what the passive voice is. You're a veteran of this book by now. You know what's coming next.

Passive aggressive

Have you been on Wikipedia at all? Of course, you have. That's not so much a single passive voice, more a great apathetic choir. And there's a good reason for that. The passive voice lets you omit the subject from a sentence, so you just end up with an object and a verb; and you do that because either you don't know about the subject so you can't write it; or the object of the sentence is actually its focus. Here's an example of this, and it's a very Wikipedia sentence.

> Slicken von Klicken **was** crowned a hundred years ago.

Passive voice, right? If we wanted to make it active, we'd put the subject first. But this sentence has no subject! I guess in this case the subject would be von Klicken's loyal robot hordes, reverently lifting the uranium circlet to his brow, but they're not what we're writing about. Because of a quirk of the verb *crowned*, the interesting noun is the subject, not the object; and a rewrite will make the sentence longer, and significantly worse. We'd need to introduce a subject where there wasn't one before, it would all just get terrible.

If you used the passive voice to elide a mysterious or boring subject, keep it like that. Here's another one.

> Von Klicken pulled a banana from his holster. He cursed. Mistakes **had been** made.

71

This is the classic way to deflect responsibility. I'm using it here for humour, although it's a pretty old joke, and not very funny. Oh and note that there's no *was* here: *had been* is doing the same job. Another, similar use, is to use the passive voice to do what it does best: deliberately introduce passivity and detachment.

> Dazed by the blow, Janet fell to her knees. She **was** being laughed at by the goat...

Here we're trying to get into Janet's head by making the writing less distinct. Honestly, I can take or leave that. I don't think it gives you much other than a lot of words. *The goat laughed at her...* is, in my opinion, much crisper. But the point is, once you understand the way the passive voice slows your narrative, you can exploit it.

Impassive

Here's a good one. How do you deal with this?

> The goat **was** enormous, and its horns blotted out the floodlights.

Was means passive voice, so I should rearrange the subject to move to the front, right? No! I was a stinky cheater, and wrote this to show you how *was* doesn't always mean we're being passive.

The trick here is that *was* actually is the verb. There's no other verbs being made passive by the presence of *was*. This is a fascinating little sentence, because *was* is really weird. (Yes, okay, you are allowed to be not fascinated by this, come, let me have my foibles.)

In this case *was* is a form of the verb *to be*. You know: *I am, you are, she is, we are...* This little blighter is radically different to most other verbs. It can use adjectives as subjects! Its infinitive looks nothing like its other forms! And, most importantly, it doesn't describe what actions are happening, it just describes what exists.

Frankly, calling it a verb is just a massive bodge to make sentences conform to the requirement to have one. But, we live in a world where we don't get to make renegade grammar systems, despite the stupidity of the one we've got: so we have to just make do, and in this sentence, *was* is the verb and the subject is *the goat* and its at the start, so its not passive. And the object is *enormous*, an adjective, and that's at the end.

I'm sorry, I'm calming down now.

The key thing here is, if you're using *was*, it might just be the verb *to be*, in which case, this sentence isn't passive, and doesn't need fixing. There's actually a few other issues with *was*, and we'll look at them later, in chapter eighteen.

Summary

The subject of a verb is the thing doing it. The object of the verb is the thing the verb is being done to. Active voice has the subject first.

 The shark sighed at the octopus.

Passive voice puts the object first, and adds in a *was* or something similar to make the sentence work.

❝ The octopus was sighed at by the shark.

It's clunkier, and there's a perception of it being less active, so it's a good idea to fix up. However, using it lets you remove the subject completely, and that can be useful if the subject isn't very interesting, or you don't know what the subject is.

❝ To her surprise, the shark's car had been fixed.

Here, the subject should be whatever had fixed the car, but we don't know, so we drop it.

Because it's used a lot in official text, it can also be used to mimic corporate-sounding pronouncements. You might be able to use it to indicate passivity, but I've not had much luck with that.

Lastly, not all sentences with *was* in them are passive. *Was* could be being used as a verb to describe something, for example.

Further reading

Janice Hardy is a writer who has written a wealth of blogs on every part of the craft, and it's worth spending some time on her site. Here she says that the passive voice is a sign that you're getting something else wrong. It's a really nice take. https://blog.janicehardy.com/2009/05/passive-aggression.html

And here's a piece that notes that you don't have to remove every instance of passive voice. https://www.ignite dinkwriting.com/ignite-your-ink-blog-for-writers/passive-voice-how-to-recognize-and-fix-it-in-creative-writing/2019

As promised, here's the Wiki page on object-verb-subject word order, or, as us grammar nerds call it, OVS. You can read how a Wikipedian tries to patiently explain that the passive voice is not, in fact, OVS. If you can understand why, you're better at grammar than I am. https://en.wikipedia.org/wiki/Object%E2%80%93verb%E2%80%93subject_word_order

Chapter 9

I wrote an ugly adjective

An exciting introduction

I've been threatening you with adjectives for some time, and now here they are, falling like a piano in a cartoon. I think of all the topics that we've covered, adjectives are the one that trip me up the most. It took me a long time to realise why, and it's a personal thing.

You know how people say that they are visual? Well, I'm the complete opposite. When I read physical descriptions in novels, it goes in one eye and out the other. I really struggle to 'see' things. Instead, I'm very auditory: I always think of things in terms of sound, and to a lesser degree, smell. So, the visual language of my text is often composed of very broad-brush things, like light and complexity and scale, and I struggle to write small visible details. Because of this I hate describing characters!

And of course, that's where adjectives pop up the most: descriptions.

Firstly, though, before we really get stuck in, we have some more grammar. Oh, yes. Concentrate, this is important.

To help us, we'll do some more examples. So, let's pick up where we left off with Sheena and Colin.

I don't know if you remember, but Colin the polar bear had just turned up with the new photocopier, and had accidentally destroyed half the storeroom. And, he's late, again: Colin has a real time management issue. He hasn't even changed out of his swimming costume, but that's okay, because he's, you know, a polar bear, and dress codes are different for them.

Anyway. As you probably remember from school, an adjective modifies a noun. This isn't strictly true, but it's a good place to start.

> Colin put down the **battered** photocopier. His **striped** bathing suit was still **wet**. He looked **miserable**.

There are four adjectives here. The first two, *battered* and *striped*, are in the place you expect adjectives to be, nestled up next to a noun. The other two, *wet* and *miserable*, are also adjectives, but they're tucked away behind a *was* and a *looked*.

The thing that the haters hate about them is that adjectives can be just word gunk; they clog the tubes of our writing engines with unnecessary letters. In this case, you could say that they have a point: knowing that the photocopier is battered and that his swim suit is striped adds

77

colour to the scene, but do we need it? Let's put together some guidelines to help.

My adjective's subjective! How does it smell? Awful!

The first and easiest are what I call 'subjective' adjectives. I mentioned these in adverbs, in chapter six. Everyone's favourite example is *beautiful*. I like to call these types of adjectives subjective because they are the writer's subjective opinion of the scene, not the reader's.

These are wrong because we're not painting beautiful word pictures that lead our readers into the majesty of our scene. Instead, we're just saying, trust me, it's awesome. This is not good.

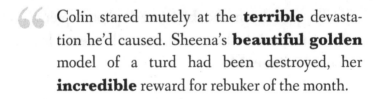

> Colin stared mutely at the **terrible** devastation he'd caused. Sheena's **beautiful golden** model of a turd had been destroyed, her **incredible** reward for rebuker of the month.

A *beautiful golden model of a turd* is something that the reader may not agree with! This is a form of telling, not showing: we're not showing its beauty, we're telling the reader about it. There's a whole galaxy of these adjectives, and they're all used to indicate that something is 'good' or 'bad.'

Our job as writers isn't to tell our reader our value judgements, because that's clumsy. Our job is to delicately show it, and lead them to the same conclusion as us. In the example above, *terrible*, *beautiful* and *incredible* are all obviously subjective. *Golden* is objective, however, so that doesn't need to be purged.

Fortunately, the fix for these is really easy: you can just delete them. The text will lose nothing.

> Colin stared mutely at the devastation he'd caused. He stood, dripping. Sheena's **golden** model of a turd had been destroyed, her reward for rebuker of the month.

There. Now, you either think, yes, this is fine, it is indeed better; or you feel that it has been a terrible loss. Well, you probably won't feel that about this passage, because the adjectives were all so obviously awful that they could go, but there are less obvious subjective adjectives.

> Sheena put her headset down. She stared at Colin, her eyes blazing with a **terrifying** rage.
>
> Colin opened his mouth. He tried to think of something **soothing** to say, but the **difficult** words just stuck in his throat.
>
> 'Good morning...?' he ventured.

These are also subjective adjectives, because what I think is *terrifying* and *soothing* and *difficult* you might not. However, here we're dipping quite close to Colin's point of view. I'm writing subjective adjectives, because I'm trying to convey his subjective experience.

I think I would change or delete *terrifying*. I'd do that

because it's very telly-not-showy, and it's not in a sentence which is about Colin's experience.

Soothing I think I would keep, because it's not very subjective and, at the end of the day, it's an important part of what he wants to do: he isn't going to say something sarcastic or funny or angry, so it's how he's seeing the world.

Difficult is sort of in the middle; but it's not doing a very useful job where it is, so let's just nix it. Generally, I think, asking if an adjective is doing anything useful is a good question. If you're on the fence, try it without and see what it looks like.

> Sheena put her headset down. She stared at Colin, her eyes blazing with rage.
>
> Colin opened his mouth. He tried to think of something **soothing** to say, but the words just stuck in his throat.
>
> 'Good morning...?' he ventured.

Now I will be the first to admit that her eyes have lost something. We'll come back to this later. How about this?

> Sheena pointed at him.
>
> 'You!' she screamed.
>
> Well this looks **awful**, thought Colin.

Awful is very subjective. But this is fine! It's fine because we're now deep in Colin's thoughts, so we're hearing what he has to say, and he can be as subjective as he likes. In fact, this is where subjective adjectives really come into their own:

you can use them to show that characters have different opinions to each other. But while characters can tell us, you the writer, need to show us, so you keep the subjective adjectives out of the narrative.

Redundant redundant redundant adjectives

When an adjective is telling us about an attribute of a noun that we know the noun definitely already has, then the adjective is redundant.

> The **sharp** shards of Sheena's award crunched under his foot. He grabbed a tube of **sticky** glue from the shelves. He held it up and tried a **happy** smile.
> 'I'm sure I can fix it!'

Shards are always sharp. Glue is always sticky. So here the *sharp* in *sharp shards* and *sticky* in *sticky glue* are redundant. Redundant adjectives are unwelcome: they are pointlessly taking up reading time when our readers are desperate to know what fate awaits poor Colin.

Now, I find I get redundancy from two places. The first is simple editing mistakes. I might be moving stuff around, I'll end up collapsing some sentences into each other and, bam, an adjective ends up with a noun where it shouldn't. That's easy. I'll just delete it, and save myself another word.

However, the second is that I'm scratching around for some emphasis and I'll settle on putting some adjectives in. Of course I know that glue is sticky, so when I write sticky glue I mean super-duper-extra-sticky. For me, this is stuff like *hot flames* or *cold ice*: it's always sensory things which I'm trying to lay on thick. These adjectives are redundant, but I want to indicate that, ouch, this is unpleasant for my character.

So, here, when I wrote *happy smile*, yes, all smiles are happy, it's redundant. But that's not what I meant. I meant that he's desperately trying to show that he is the happiest polar bear there is, everything is fine, everything can be fixed.

> The shards of Sheena's award crunched under his foot. He grabbed a tube of glue from the shelves. He held it up and tried **his happiest** smile.
>
> 'I'm sure I can fix it!'

This isn't redundant any more. I deleted the first two, and fixed the third. Smiles are always happy: however, this is the *happiest smile*, and so it's showing that he's really grinning as hard as he can, desperate to fix the devastation and his relationship with Sheena.

Yes, it's not redundant any more. It's also, if we're going to be honest, rather weak. So we're back to adverbs: perhaps this is a weakness of my text which I'm patching over with adjectives.

> The shards of Sheena's award crunched under his foot. He grabbed a tube of glue from the shelves.

'I'm sure I can fix it!' he said, trying his best impression of **cheerful** competency.

I messed about with this a little. I even considered an adverb-as-art (*smiled bleakly*) but it wasn't doing it for me. *Cheerful* is quite a nice adjective because he's clearly not cheerful.

My adjective was a red-hot cliche

This is the third and final type in our trilogy: cliched adjectives.

As I keep saying, writing is hard. Everything has been thought of by someone before us. People have been writing for thousands of years, and they are writing in ever greater numbers today. How are we supposed to be original? It's not fair.

Nevertheless, that is what your cheering readership expects. And they are indeed cheering: they're all outside, chanting your name, right now. I can hear them. So, we're not going to let them down with a cliché, are we?

There are cliches everywhere across writing: characters, plots, scenarios, settings, dialogue, you name it. When you read them you'll groan with recognition. However, nowhere is the cliché more obvious than here, down at the word level. You can take age-old plots and twist or disguise them. Your characters can have old tropes mixed in a new way. But when we see an adjective next to a noun, and we've seen that pair a million times before, it's impossible to hide it. It's just there. Yes, this is true for lots of other parts of writing, adverbs in particular; but for me, it's the adjectives which are the battleground against cliché.

Try this.

> Colin retreated from Sheena's **blazing fury**, knocking over a case of printer ink in his haste.
>
> 'You... Did... This!' she screamed, punctuating each word with a jab from her **shaking finger**.
>
> 'I'll work late to tidy it,' replied Colin. 'Look, I'll move the photocopier now.'
>
> He tried to pick up the machine, but his **sharp claws** tore through the beige plastic. **Thick smoke** poured out.
>
> Sheena doubled up, coughing.
>
> 'Mmmm. I think this might be getting a little warm,' said Colin.
>
> He ran his paw over the photocopier. It wasn't just warm: it was **red hot**.
>
> Might be time for a **quick exit**, thought Colin.

These adjectives aren't subjective or redundant. Well, *sharp claws* is actually rather redundant, because claws are generally sharp, although I guess some animals have sharper claws than others. But how many times have you read those adjective-noun pairs before? *Blazing fury, shaking finger, sharp claws, thick smoke, red hot, quick exit. Red hot* is particularly egregious: we've seen that many, many times before. If it was literally glowing red, well, then I guess it would be okay because that's not a metaphor, it's a literal statement of fact. But, here, it's not.

Warm welcomes, long nights, wide eyes, innocent bystanders. You've seen them all before. Our readers don't want to read them again! They're after startling novelty which will cause them to drop to their knees and weep at the clarity and originality of the prose.

So what do we do?

I'm sure you'll be shocked and astonished when I say that your first option is to delete the adjective. Well, probably not that shocked or astonished given that's all I've been saying for a few pages now. Let's try that.

> Colin retreated from Sheena's **fury**, knocking over a case of printer ink in his haste.
>
> 'You... Did... This!' she screamed, punctuating each word with a jab from her **finger**.
>
> 'I'll work late to tidy it,' replied Colin. 'Look, I'll move the photocopier now.'
>
> He tried to pick up the machine, but his **claws** tore through the beige plastic. **Smoke** poured out.
>
> Sheena doubled up, coughing.
>
> 'Mmmm. I think this might be getting a little warm,' said Colin.
>
> He ran his paw over the photocopier. It wasn't just warm: it was **hot**.
>
> Might be time for a **quick exit**, thought Colin.

So I removed all but *quick* from *quick exit*. *Might be time for an exit* doesn't sound right. That's going to need a full rewrite if I want to get rid of that.

With the rest gone, though, it hasn't lost much. I thought I'd miss the *sharp* but actually it's fine: we can infer that his claws are sharp through his actions, so I guess that was redundant after all.

Clarifying tall adjectives and short adjectives

I've spent a lot of time talking about when to remove adjectives. This feels unfair. They can be useful little things, after all. The one time they absolutely get a free ride is when our (objective, non-redundant, non-cliched) adjectives are being used to clarify things.

If you don't mind us leaving Colin for a little while, we'll go to Janet.

> Janet crept closer. The body was spread-eagled across the roof.
>
> Two robot goons were standing over it. The **taller** one looked down over it, a sneer fixed to its **metal** face. The **smaller** one stared out across the city. It took out a cigarette and lit it.

Here, I distinguish between two unknown and otherwise identical characters using adjectives, *taller* and *smaller*. I clarify the text because the only way to tell which character is which, in this case, is through the adjectives. Oh, I put the *metal* in *metal face* because it made me happy.

This particular scene seems to be a thing we see in thrillers, where our hero overhears unknown low-level baddies.

The problem with this is that these adjectives are almost working too hard. If you have any extended narration of these two characters, you're going to be using them a lot. You'll see the same word over and over again and it will be tiresome.

I'm not much of a thriller writer, but I think that a few things tend to happen to stop the overuse of clarifying adjectives.

> **Shorty** flicked his cigarette over the edge of the building. It spiralled downwards, and sparks flew from its tip.

Here we replaced *the short robot* with a nickname. This nickname is supposed to be given by the protagonist as they stare, hidden, in a wheelie bin; but the narrator will use it from here on. I think this works better in first person than in third, where the lines between the narrator and the protagonist are much more blurred.

The next is to have them give their names in dialogue. It's hard not to make this sound forced.

> 'I say **Eustace**, old bean. You should cut down that jolly nasty habit,' said the **taller** one. 'It'll kill you, don't you know.'

'Right-ho, **Tristram**. I say, have you seen that cad Janet around at all? We need to give her a ruddy good hiding if we find her,' replied Eustace.

Yes, okay, I didn't help myself in the whole 'sound forced' stakes. But the fact is, people don't use each other's names so much in real speech, so this will always sound clunky. There are other, equally contrived ways of achieving this: name badges, uniform patches, cyberpunk hacking. But having introduced names you then no longer have to use clarifying adjectives.

However, by far the easiest way of dealing with this situation is a blizzard of bullets.

> Janet stepped out and fired. The robots collapsed, cogs rolling out from their torsos.
> I wonder who they were, she thought.

I suppose characters in that sort of a scenario are fairly disposable.

Huh, we went on rather a long diversion. The point here is that adjectives that are used to clarify the text are useful, but they should be nice straightforward ones, and obviously not subjective, redundant or cliched.

And if you need them to distinguish things, you may have written yourself into a bit of a hole, so backtracking and figuring out a way out might be a good idea: why do you have two objects or people which can only be distinguished through adjectives? The whole thing above with two anonymous baddies talking to each other before being killed off is kind of lazy.

Having said that, clarifying adjectives are fine if they're not used for very long.

> Sheena staggered out of the room, coughing. The fire alarm wailed. Colin opened a side panel on the photocopier.
>
> Now, which wire am I supposed to cut? Is it the **red one** or the **blue one**? Oh, I wish I'd watched that movie more carefully...

Gosh darn ostra-flipping-nenie

But I want to use adjectives! I like them!

Well, in that case, we make our adjectives amazing. We want them to be surprising and descriptive. A good adjective makes the scene jump out; it reduces ambiguity, and it introduces a texture to the writing which wasn't there before. If you wish to amaze your friends and awe your enemies, there's a fantastic technical term for this: it's called 'ostranenie.' It's all about how you can make the familiar seem new, how you can introduce strangeness in the mundane. Yes, we want to see some gosh darn ostra-flipping-nenie in our writing.

> He ran his claw over its control panel. The machine's alarm had triggered, and it was making a **high, melancholic wail**. Its little screen was a tapestry of **wistful symbols**,

each one indicating that nothing would ever be the same again.

I think I should throw this switch right here, Colin thought. That should do it.

The machine shivered before going silent, the smoke ceasing.

Colin sat back, relieved. That actually could have been worse, he thought.

The machine emitted a single **apologetic beep**; the alarm resumed. This time it was **gleeful**.

'Self-destruct initiated,' said the display.

Oh dear.

This is where my limitations as a writer are showing. I've tried to use surprising adjectives. I went for ostranenie! Alarms have no emotion, and so are not *melancholic, apologetic* or *gleeful*. Photocopier display icons are not *wistful*. Now by using these, I've almost broken POV, and we'll talk about that in chapter twelve, but I think that actually we both know that the photocopier doesn't have a point of view, it's just something that Colin is perceiving.

What we're aiming for is that perfect adjective which makes them stop and go, huh. That's new. I never thought about photocopiers that way. We want to pull our readers into particular directions, by associating things with other things in surprising ways.

And ideally, it doesn't make them stop; instead, they're swept up with the narrative, and the whole thing is lucid raindrops of text sparkling all around them, gentle, clear, and perfect.

Like Colin's tears. Poor Colin.

But beware of purple! This is something we'll see in chapter seventeen.

I actually used another type of adjective earlier, and tried to hide it. Let's go back.

> He tried to pick up the machine, but his claws tore through the **beige plastic**.

Beige plastic is, I think, inherently funny, because these days the only things which are that are ancient pieces of office technology. You write on a laptop described as oblivion black or nova white or regret grey or some other such wildly over-the-top, ostranenic (no that is not a word) colour adjective. With *beige plastic*, I'm going for the humour of the mundane. So this isn't hit-you-like-a-sack-of-frogs beauty or funny, this is just a tiny bit of silly.

The lesson here is that I'm thinking carefully about my adjectives. That means when I use them I've put a little piece of art into my sentence. They aren't things to just churn out thoughtlessly. They are precious things to be placed carefully.

As good as a simile

So, adjectives are hard, and have to earn their keep. How do we describe things if we want to avoid them? We have a few tricks.

Your friend *like* (and also its posh relative *as*) is an excellent adjective substitute. When we say a thing is like another thing, we are using a 'simile.' They describe something without using descriptive words at all.

> Colin, **smoking like a kipper** and **screaming like a k-pop fan**, hurtled out of the photocopier repair room. It exploded behind him, **paper fluttering down like confetti**, the walls splattered with ink.

Look, ma, no adjectives, and yet you know exactly what's going on, with plenty of colour. Similes are a powerful way to describe things: they tend not to be subjective, just because of their construction. They can let you be artistic: you can insert startling and beguiling language into your text.

Similes are not free of problems, however. In particular, beware of cliches. How many times have you read *big as a house? Light as a feather?* These take four precious words and give us nothing other than a vague sense of despair that we had to read them yet again.

> Colin flew **like a bird** out of the office window. He landed on the pavement **like a sack of spuds**. Pedestrians darted back, as **quick as lightning**, gasping. They were not used to aerial polar bears.

Each of those three similes are cliches and bog down our precious text. Even when the similes are wonderful, you can get echoing on the word *like* (which we'll cover in chapter thirteen), so you should be very light with them. When they are not wonderful, or you're saying *like* more than an eighties teen, let's just delete them.

> Colin flew out of the office window. He landed on the pavement. Pedestrians darted back, gasping. They were not used to aerial polar bears.

Unlike adjectives, it's not free to delete similes: the rhythm of this is now all off. *He landed on the pavement* feels very abrupt: I think I'd probably change it to something like *He landed on the pavement and groaned.*

All in

One last technique, and we're done. Adjectives not good enough for you? Similes don't have that zing? This is it: this is the bazooka that you keep under the desk for those special moments. It's called an 'adjectival phrase' and it's when we use an entire clause instead of an adjective.

> The silence was broken by a cough.
> Colin opened his eyes a fraction. Standing above him, **radiant with the fury of a thousand burning modems**, was Sheena.
> 'Hello?' tried Colin.

I could have said *Sheena was standing above him, furious.* But I didn't. This is a pivotal point in my story. An adjectival phrase is a phrase which we can use instead of an adjective. It is the ultimate gambit: I can stick long, rambling text in there, and it will modify my noun. I am taking all my poker chips and pushing them to the centre of the table. I sit back in my chair while the crowd gasps around me. This is the place I made Sheena's eyes blaze terrifyingly, and I didn't use any subjective adjectives at all.

As an aside, note the passive voice used in that sentence: *Standing above him* [...] *was Sheena*. I structured it that way so that the punchline of the sentence was at the end. Looking at it again, I'm not sure that this is the best way of putting it together. I could try other ways. There is a degree of compromise to these things: sometimes you can't find the single perfect configuration. Try things.

All adjectival phrases follow the same pattern. They have a so-called 'head' adjective, which is the thing you're replacing. Then all the rest rolls along with it. They can have adverbs, but I think we've talked enough about them, and you don't need me to dig up that robot-vampire-filled grave. You can use all sorts of structures. Similes are, of course, an adverbial phrase, but there are others too.

> The fumes billowed around them both, **stinking with his despair**. His misery, **hot and sharp**, overflowed from him. Tears ran down his cheeks, only partly invoked by the smoke.

Stinking with his despair is an adjectival phrase. Head adjective is *stinking*. *Hot and sharp* is also one, because lists of adjectives are adjectival phrases, and I guess either could be the head adjective.

Try taking an adjective, using it as the head adjective and playing with it to see what you get. *Miserable?* How about *misery soaked?* That's interesting, because the lead adjective then is *soaked. Terrified?* What about *drenched with terror?* Yeah, I'm riding the water analogies here, but you get the idea.

As with all such dramatic gestures, you're laying it on thick here, so beware of purple! I've mentioned the chapter about eleven times, here it is again, chapter seventeen.

The end

Look, I'll be honest. I just wanted to finish the story.

> I can't do this any more, thought Colin. It's not for me. I'm the only photocopier repair polar bear I know. Heck, I'm the only polar bear I know, period. I can't work in an office.
>
> He pulled himself to his feet. Sheena was screaming. Her words spilled over him in an **incoherent** torrent, **like the scraps of paper** that fluttered down from the **smashed** window above.
>
> His muscles ached, his eyes burned. He faced her, staring down her **volcanic** rage.
>
> 'Sheena,' he said, and he didn't hide his polar bear voice, didn't try to **squeak like a human**. The sound rumbled around the street,

low and despondent. Sheena snapped her mouth closed, **like a puppet**.
    'Sheena: I quit.'
    He turned and walked away.
    Behind him, the crowd cheered.

Here we have two clarifying adjectives: *incoherent* and *smashed*. One surprising adjective: *volcanic*. Two similes which are rooted in the story: *like the scraps of paper* and *like a human*. One simile which is unrelated to anything else: *like a puppet*. Then an adjectival phrase, *low and despondent*.

This is probably about right.

Summary

Adjectives are precious things. Don't let them be subjective, redundant or cliched.

Subjective adjectives are things like *beautiful* or *horrible*: they are the subjective opinion of the narrator, not the objective description of the scene.

Redundant adjectives aren't needed because they describe properties of things we already know: *green grass* or *hot flames* or *transparent glass*.

Cliched adjectives are ones we've seen many times before: *warm welcome* or *innocent bystanders*.

Clarifying adjectives are things which make the text clearer. For example, they might be distinguishing between *the taller building* and *the shorter building*, because we can see both. However, overuse might indicate a systemic problem.

Adjectives which are surprising and eloquent can be tiny pieces of art in our writing, and we love them. But they are precious, and not to be strewn around.

Similes are when we describe something by comparing it to something else. They are often of the form *thing is like other thing,* or *something as something.* For example, *as hot as the sun.* They are as precious as good adjectives and can be wonderful. When overused they make the text worse. When cliched, they make the text much worse.

Adjectival phrases are great, but are heavy and slow and may be better for special moments.

Beware of purple prose.

Further reading

Here's a piece by a writer called Emma Darwin. I like some of the extra caveats that she puts in, particularly around what she calls 'psychic distance.' https://emmadarwin.typepad. com/thisitchofwriting/2017/11/cut-all-the-adjectives- adverbs-why-its-nonsense-and-why-it-isnt.html

Here's a wonderful piece about adjectives which will teach you all sorts of useless information which you can use to impress your friends and awe your enemies. https://www. nytimes.com/2007/03/11/books/chapters/0311-1st- yago.html

Lastly, I mentioned that you make compromises with yourself. The end result is that, when you look back at your work, you will only see the faults. This is known as 'harp- maker's cornea' and is documented here. https://wonder mark.com/c/c1529/

Chapter 10

I wrote a sentence it was a run-on sentence

Unclear fusion

We did adjectives! Everyone, take a moment. Yeah.

This one is nice and easy, and you should be able to read this one while, I don't know, mowing the lawn? Fighting the troll king? Smooching the handsome prince or princess? All three at once?

Anyway, this time we're going to treat ourselves to run-on sentences. Show rather than tell: here's a run-on. This is a common-or-garden 'fused' run-on.

> Gallagher scrawled his name on the bomb the penguins played their crazy melody.

The fused run-on is nice and easy, because it's so obviously wrong. We can see that it's two clauses badly welded together. And that's all a run-on is: it's a sentence which has been improperly assembled from smaller component sentences. A fused one is where they just got slammed into each other, and left, smoking.

> The water surged surged surged it fell on him like despair.

This one is as obviously wrong, but might be artistic? I think this is a style for your second novel, after your first has sold a zillion copies and has had rave reviews and you've appeared on the covers of all the magazines (including *Tractors and the People Who Drive Them*) and can do no wrong as an author; because you're not going to get away with it for your first, I'm afraid.

One more example:

> The zombies roved outside **nevertheless** Gallagher still worked on the wiring.

This is still a fused run-on, but the *nevertheless* might trick you. The thing that's going on here is that *nevertheless* is being used as a conjunction. A conjunction is a word like *and* or *but,* and it joins two things together. However, *nevertheless* is not a conjunction! It's an adverb. (*Steven King will eat it nevertheless.*) Using it to fuse two sentences makes a run-on. If I put in a real conjunction, you can see how much nicer it looks.

> The zombies roved outside, **but** Gallagher still worked on the wiring.

A rule of thumb is that you can look for fused run-ons by saying them out loud: they have a funny flatness to them which makes them easy to spot.

So how do we fix?

It's pretty obvious. We either split into the sub-sentences, or we fix the join. Splitting is easy. Stick a full stop in, boom.

> Gallagher scrawled his name on the bomb. The penguins played their crazy melody.

Fixing the join is harder, and is something I get wrong a lot. Your three options are a semicolon, or a conjunction and a comma, or a conjunction without the comma. Compare and contrast.

> Gallagher scrawled his name on the bomb; the penguins played their crazy melody.

> Gallagher scrawled his name on the bomb, **and** the penguins played their crazy melody.

> Gallagher scrawled his name on the bomb **while** the penguins played their crazy melody.

More conjunctions, but I'm not going into them just yet. Instead, I'm going to step into the bloody arena of the semicolons. Because this is fun: it's when the knives get picked up. Should you semicolon or not? In my experience, this has the highest chance of any topic of inducing stabbing-in-the-throat-with-a-fork level arguments between writers. Why? Because it's deeply personal, we all have different opinions, and everyone's basically correct.

Before we go there, though, I'm going to give you a very quick reminder of how semicolons work.

Hemi semi demi colons

There are a few uses of semicolons, but the one that we're interested in is when you take two sentences and you glue them together. So:

> Gallagher dragged the bomb into the main room. Its metal casing shrieked on the concrete floor.

These are two related sentences. This means they're a perfect candidate for joining with a semicolon. How do you do that? Easy. You just throw away the full stop, replace it with a semicolon, and fix up the case.

> Gallagher dragged the bomb into the main room; its metal casing shrieked on the concrete floor.

That's it. I changed the full stop into a semi, and I lower-cased the *Its* into *its*. You don't need conjunctions or anything else.

Now by doing this I'm signalling that the two events are closely linked in some way; you shouldn't really semicolon link things together which are unrelated.

To semi or not to semi; that is the question

As noted, you can fix fused run-ons with semicolons.

> The zombies roved outside nevertheless Gallagher still worked on the wiring.

This becomes

> The zombies roved outside; nevertheless, Gallagher still worked on the wiring.

You can see how easy it was. I put the semicolon in, and then it needed the coma in too. Because I was fixing a fused run-on rather than splicing two sentences together, there wasn't even upper case letters to fix. Semicolons are definitely nice and terse.

If you go without, you're supposed to use a conjunction with a comma, and that adds one extra word.

> Gallagher scrawled his name on the bomb; the penguins played their crazy melody.

> Gallagher scrawled his name on the bomb, and the penguins played their crazy melody.

In terms of sheer numbers of characters, this is the shortest way of fixing run-ons.

But my, some people hate semicolons. There is an argument – and, I think, a compelling one – that the little things alienate some people from your writing. Because some of its other rules are tricksy (and they are more than just breaking up run-ons) and people get them wrong, and dang it, we just don't see 'em in picture books like we do all the rest of punctuation, we're excluding some people's enjoyment. Will your readers throw your book across the room in frustration when they see them? Maybe? Maybe not?

Nowhere is this more debate heated than in dialogue. Should you use semicolons in speech? I've seen a man tumbling down a London Underground escalator, blood fountaining from his neck, because he advocated just that. (When he landed, he came to a full stop. I'm so sorry.) The argument here is that no one pronounces semicolons, so you should never use them when recounting what people say. They will prevent you from writing fluid dialogue.

And yet, and yet, they are so great for a certain kind of pause...

I ran an extremely unscientific study. I grabbed random paperbacks from my bookshelf and flicked through, looking for semicolons in direct speech. I had a lot of US and UK authors, but not so many from other places, so please forgive me if that's what you write. My results were that the older and more British the book was, the more likely it was to use them. So if you're writing for American kids? Probably avoid in dialogue. Writing for grumpy old Brits (hello!)? Maybe okay to keep 'em. Certainly the reigning king of semicolons in dialogue is George Bernard Shaw (grumpy old Brit, check), who used them like they were going out of fashion... Which I guess they did?

I, personally, like them. But I also accept that for a certain audience they aren't correct. You need to do two things: the first is establish your narrative voice, and the voice of your characters, and this is definitely a part of that. The second is that you need to read recent trad published books in your genre and get a feeling for what's correct there. Ideally it will be debut books, because those authors went through what you want to go through. Scrutinize sentence structure, look at the punctuation.

Comma feel the noise

If you try and get the best of both worlds, by dropping the conjunction and using a comma on its own, you end up with a different kind of run-on sentence: it's a 'comma spliced' run-on sentence, because we have two sentences improperly spliced together by a comma.

> Gallagher scrawled his name on the bomb, the penguins played their crazy melody.

Now, everyone will be enraged when they read that sentence. However, half are enraged that it's allowed; the other half are enraged that it's forbidden. Me, I just want to get through the week without finding venomous animals in my underwear drawer, so point your murderous fury somewhere else, yeah? But the fact is, by the rules of grammar, that's really not fine. You shouldn't do this.

And yet, it looks kind of okay. My theory with comma spliced sentences is that your brain expects them to be the first two elements of a list. So this is completely legit:

> Gallagher scrawled his name on the bomb, the penguins played their crazy melody, **and** the world outside burned.

(Gosh, this chapter the example sentences are bleak, aren't they? Normal service will be resumed soon, I promise...)

This isn't a run-on, because this is a conjunction plus some commas: it just so happens that the conjunction *and* is mighty, and can carry many other clauses on its sturdy shoulders, all joined with commas, so the first clause gets to tag along for free. I think it's such a standard sight that we can cope with comma spliced run-ons quite naturally, it's like you've elided an *and*.

Because of the missing conjunction, comma splices have a lazy, sloppy feel: when you use them, it's like you're listening to a stoned hippy with opinions. That's a thing, but maybe not a thing to use.

You fix comma spliced run-ons exactly the same way you fixed fused run ons: with semicolons, or conjunctions, or full stops.

And poly put the synd and on

There is one last kind of thing called a run-on. The gloriously named 'polysyndeton' run-on is a sentence that is just using too many dang *and*s. That's not actually true, although that's probably the type that you'll see the most. It's actually a sentence which has stitched lots of clauses together using coordinating conjunctions.

Conjunctions are little words that join together clauses in sentences. The seven coordinating conjunctions are the ones everyone knows. They are *and, but, for, nor, or, so,* and *yet.* As far as grammar is concerned, you can chain them pretty much indefinitely and when you do, you get a poly-syndeton.

> The zombies howled, **and** a hot wind blew, **and** the city lit up brighter than the sun, **and** finally everything was silent, **and** ash fell from the sky.

In the above example, it reads a bit like Molly Bloom's chapter in *Ulysses*; it definitely needs some cutting up. But, polysyndetons are not all bad: they have a heavy ponderous-ness to them. They are relentless and emphatic and pitiless. They feel like that because each clause has an equal weight to them, so you have this sort of plodding march. They're used a lot as a rhetorical device, but of course what works for the spoken word doesn't translate so much to the page. We've gone from the delicate dance of textured prose to heavy drumbeat.

Unlike the other run-ons we've been discussing these are technically fine. You have to use them with purpose, though. The example above is not a very good polysyndeton: I'm telling a story but some of the clauses happen at the same time, and some follow one another. And that means the polysyndeton gets in the way of your understanding of what's going on. Polysyndetons – you know what, I think I'm fed up of typing that, I'm going to call then polys – are best used when all the things joined together are of the same sort.

> Gallagher looked across the storeroom, taking it all in, letting the memories wash into him. This was my life for so long, he thought. I don't know how I can leave.
>
> He picked up a wrench.
>
> I used this to fix a water leak the first time I found this place.
>
> The penguins were playing their moon ballad, up on the church roof. He closed his eyes and it filled his ears for the last time.
>
> Because with the dust **and** the despair **and** the pain **and** the endless, endless loneliness... They're too much. I can't stay here.

I'm using the poly to emphasise the things he wants to escape. It's a list where all the elements are of the same type, and so it's more focused than the last one.

Then I stopped using then

Yes, it's true. This last thing is not about run-ons. However, it fits here quite nicely.

It's easy: don't use *then* too much.

> Gallagher returned the wrench to the shelf. **Then**, he put his jacket on. **Then** he walked to the door. He opened it, and stared out at the

wasteland beyond. **Then** he walked through, off to his new life.

This is purposefully a bit ludicrous. But it does highlight the problem: the overuse of *then* makes it sound like children's writing.

You almost never need *then*. We use it to show that actions follow each other, but, actually, our readers can figure that out. It's almost the opposite to the whole *start/begin* thing: our incredible human brains can figure this out without needing those additional cues.

> Gallagher returned the wrench to the shelf. He put his jacket on, and walked to the door. He opened it, and stared out at the wasteland beyond.
>
> He took a breath and held it; and walked through, off to his new life.

I've heard people say to never use *then*. That might be going too far, but it's both very boring and often redundant. Plus, of course, it's an adverb, and we all know what we think about them.

Summary

Run-ons! These are sentences that are made of things rammed together when they perhaps shouldn't be. You can generally tell a run-on because its rhythm sounds off when you read it out loud.

Fused run-ons are when the clauses are just mashed into each other.

> 66 Gallagher grabbed a penguin it squeaked with happiness.

There are three ways of fixing. Split into a pair of sentences:

> 66 Gallagher grabbed a penguin. It squeaked with happiness.

Split with a semicolon:

> 66 Gallagher grabbed a penguin; it squeaked with happiness.

Split with a conjunction and maybe a comma:

> 66 Gallagher grabbed a penguin, and it squeaked with happiness.

Some people don't like semicolons, particularly in dialogue. Using them is a thing which might make your work feel too inaccessible. Read recent books in your genre to decide.

Comma spliced run-ons are when you have two or more clauses joined with just commas, and no conjunctions.

> 66 The penguin wriggled, it was very slippery.

They are also wrong. You fix them the same way as fused run-ons.

Polysyndeton run-ons are sentences with many conjunctions.

> The penguin rolled and writhed and lunged and lurched; but Gallagher packed it into the travel crate.

Unlike the other two types, they can be grammatically correct so you don't need to delete them. However, they need to be purposeful. Don't overuse them, and make sure that all the clauses are related.

Then is not strictly to do with run-ons, but sometimes it gets used incorrectly as a conjunction. We generally don't like it because it looks childish, and it's mostly unnecessary.

Further reading

The best place on the internet to understand the dread semicolon is this cartoon by The Oatmeal: https://theoatmeal.com/comics/semicolon

Eats Shoots and Leaves by Lynne Truss is an excellent book on punctuation, and so contains information about semicolons, and a lot of other stuff as well.

Chapter 11

You tell them about point of view

I started with first person

This is another intermission chapter. I've mentioned point of view — or as we like to call it, POV — a few times already. We're going to get gritty with it, but before I do that I wanted to make sure you have the full background. It's a surprisingly complicated subject, but it's huge fun.

Point of view is the lens through which the reader interacts with your main characters. It's the voice that the book is written in. It doesn't have to be constant: it might vary as you jump to different narrators, or even to the same narrator in different circumstances. The choices you make will impact how that your reader responds to your work, both consciously and subconsciously, because it's the voice of the story, the window into your world.

Better writers than me have written about this, and you should go and read them as it's a huge topic. To start with, though, we're going to talk about what point of view actually is.

We'll start with first person. In this POV, you're directly in the head of the protagonist.

> **I** threw open the frosty hatch and climbed down into the cake bunker. The ovens were blazing away, warming the room and filling it with the smell of baking. **I** took **my** gloves off and let the heat seep into my hands.
>
> This was going to be a good day.

Remember pronouns? They are words like *she, I, they*. Well, first person uses *I* as the pronoun to describe the main character, because the narrating character is also the narrator. Note how in the above passage I mixed a bit of description with some inner voice: we're so close to the character that their thoughts can just leak into the text. We see their opinions and observations, directly.

Now, you don't have to stay in one person's head; writing in first person doesn't restrict you to a single character. However, if you jump to someone else, you're expected to put a chapter or section break. If you don't do that, and so you jump with no warning, it's called head-hopping or breaking point of view.

This is a rule so firm that it should be written in stone and inscribed on mountains. Always stay in one person's head until a section or chapter break! Do not head-hop! Never! Ever!

Head hopping is confusing and taxing for your readers,

because they're thrown around into another perspective without warning. It's really really obvious in first, so let's take a look.

> I put on oven gloves and pulled out a tray of cupcakes. They smelt of cinnamon and summer and hope. I tipped them onto a cooling tray.
>
> Mrs Miggins came in from the radar room. Her vampiric tendencies had abated somewhat. I thought she might be more interested in the cakes than, say, my neck.
>
> I wasn't, though. I could read that silly little snot's thoughts like a picture book: and not a very interesting or well-written one, at that. I could just imagine sinking my teeth into his arteries, draining his delicious crimson blood from his feeble corpse, the red stuff pumping from his writhing body...
>
> I shivered and smiled.
>
> 'Mmm, that smells nice.'

I jumped from one head to the other with no break. It's like a whiplash, isn't it? Plus, we're not entirely certain who is telling the story when the switch happens. Bear this in mind when we start looking at other points of view: when you head-hop in them, the strain is still there, even if you don't notice it so much.

The other thing is that head-hopping is a signifier. It signals that you are someone who head-hops, and therefore are a novice at the craft. It might seem unfair... but, yeah, critical readers are looking for this.

Back to first person: there's a lot of debate about it. It tends to be more popular in books aimed at younger audiences, and the romance genre. I've heard various passionate arguments for and against it, I have no opinions... However, we're line editing now, so you made that decision when you wrote your early drafts.

You looked at second person

Second person is when the protagonist uses the pronoun *you*. It's used for a niche set of things. The one you may be most familiar with is those game books that were cool in the eighties, like *Choose Your Own Adventure* or *Fighting Fantasy* (or if you want to be a real hipster about it, *Lone Wolf*, which was absolutely the best of the bunch). YOU are the hero. You walk into a room and fall down a pit, you are dead, go back to paragraph one.

In those, it's used very much like first person. In fact, you could write a first person story and pretty much swap the *I*s with the *you*s and you'd end up with appropriate text for a game book.

You also see it used in more serious literary fiction; my favourite is *If on a Winter's Night a Traveller* by Italo Calvino. This manages half a novel using second person, which is quite a feat, given second wears out its welcome very quickly. As a result, you'll sometimes see second in shorter works, which get to be more adventurous with these sorts of things.

Second person is weird. Look, I doubt that you're writing in it, I don't have any great wisdom here, let's move on.

She used third person

Third person is the workhorse of fiction. It uses *he, she, they, it*.

Because it's used everywhere it has a number of subtypes. I'm going to cut it between three flavours: third person omniscient, third person limited, and third person deep. This is, like all things writing, a thing that writers will argue about, and you can find any number of blogs cutting it other ways.

Omniscient is the easiest. In true third person omniscient, the narrator is everywhere all at once. We're all familiar with third omniscient in fairy tales. *Once upon a time there was a cobbler who had three hedgehogs...* The narrative jumps around characters and tells us what each one of them are thinking without breaking into a sweat.

Even in modern literature it's an older style of writing: *Under Milk Wood* by Dylan Thomas is a great example. Thomas's 'Voices' flit from head to head, looking into the minds of both sides of a conversation, telling us what everyone is thinking, remembering, hoping for, despairing about. I've heard that *The Old Man and the Sea* by Ernest Hemingway is true omniscient, too, although I've never read it and I'm not one of those people who lies about reading books to impress you.

Generally, you're not going to be writing in omniscient. It's difficult for unseasoned authors to pull off and most modern readers find it incredibly hard to engage with (unless you're reading *The Book Thief* by Markus Zuzak). Omniscient narration in novels is generally not that satisfying to read: we like being close to characters, rooting for individuals in difficult situations.

As a result, we'll aim to end up in one person's mind for the duration of a section or chapter. In that world, we're limited to that person's thoughts. This is called third person limited, the workhorse of commercial fiction.

> Isidora sank into the bar seat, Liang opposite her.
>
> Oh, it's nice to be back on the ship, she thought.
>
> Sunil followed her, carrying three tall glasses of something very alcoholic. There were far more straws and bits of fruit than she normally liked in a drink. But, given what she'd seen today, this was fine.
>
> Sunil set them down on the table, and passed one to her and Liang.
>
> 'Here's to another planetary mission where we wore red shirts and didn't get shot,' he said.

Here, I'm in Isidora's head. She's musing about drinks. I have no idea what Sunil and Liang are thinking, because of the limited third point of view. And, if I did, it would be head-hopping.

Now, it might be that you think that head-hopping in third is less jarring than first (although, I promise you that once you notice it, it still jars more than a jam factory). It's still wrong, though. Look how the narrative sort of washes in and out of her perception, like the *glasses of something* part. That's the narrator telling us what she's thinking despite not using a *she thought* tag. As a result, a head-hop in third will be disconcerting when you encounter these little not-quite-in-but-not-quite-out-of-head sentences.

Third person deep is the last one. Strictly this is a type of third limited: you're still in one person's head, using *he/she/they/it*. However, the difference is that the narrator's voice is the character's voice. In that respect we're full circle back to first person.

> Isidora sank into the bar seat, Liang opposite her.
>
> Oh, it's nice to be back on the ship, she thought.
>
> Sunil followed her, carrying three tall glasses of... something.
>
> Well, okay. There's far too many straws and bits of fruit there. But, fine, whatever, it will get me hammered. And after today, after those horrible furry things... I need it.
>
> Sunil set them down on the table, and passed one to her and Liang. The glass was cold, and the sugar around its rim crunched invitingly.
>
> 'Here's to another planetary mission where we wore red shirts and didn't get shot,' he said.

It's got a different feel to it, hasn't it? There's no ambiguity in the narrative here; we're hearing Isidora with nothing between us and her. Head-hopping here would be even more jarring.

You might feel that third deep seems artificial, because we can hear the inner voice of our main character, but we use external pronouns. Well, buckle up, buttercup: every narrative voice is artificial. Where is that first person narrator sat while they dictate seven young adult novels? Do they ever say, yeah, sorry, give me a moment, I've gotta stand up: given myself a wedgie. Nope. In third person does the voice ever stop for a paragraph to get a sandwich? Also, nope. The biggest suspension of disbelief that your reader does is to imagine that your narrative voice is a gate into a world that they are interacting with.

When good POV goes bad

A common theme is that we show what our characters are like, by telling our reader what they're thinking. Now, there are a few ways that this can go wrong.

Sometimes we haven't fully fleshed our characters out. We'll probably write them rather more distantly than we perhaps should. This is a huge topic, and not a line edit thing, but it is definitely a thing. I've done it myself.

So, if you find yourself with an unsatisfying POV, ask yourself: do I actually know what makes my character tick? What would they think if they missed a bus, bit into a bad apple, unexpectedly bumped into an ex, found buried treasure, read a book on line editing? It might be that you're skating on the edge of a deeper POV because you don't fully understand them.

Or maybe your character is someone you don't enjoy spending time with. This is tricky, because difficult characters introduce tension and drama: but very difficult characters are hard to empathise with. And, at the end of the day, your readers are driven by point of view, particularly in longer works. You can get away with quite shallow or nasty characters in short fiction, but in a novel you need that engagement.

Isolated, insular characters can be very tiring to read; they are happy living in their own heads, but we want to get out and see the world, even if they don't. Whiny characters, cruel characters, endlessly sarcastic characters: there are so many ways to make someone's mind an unpleasant place to be. So, you end up skirting around their points of view rather than going deep and showing us their complete humanity.

At the end of the day, we're writing to entertain. Unsympathetic points of view will make it harder to achieve that, and tweaking your character to make your point of view easier is often the right thing to do.

Further reading

The Emotional Craft of Fiction by Donald Maas is a really excellent read. He talks about a lot of different ways that you can build emotion, and how that's affected by the point of view you choose.

Then, here's a great blog about deep third. https:// foxprinteditorial.com/2023/06/15/deep-third-pov-manag ing-its-challenges/ This addresses the various ways you can go in and out when you use actually quite weird point of view.

I also, as always, advocate that you read fiction closely and analyse how the author is hooking you into that particular character's POV.

Chapter 12

He was obviously breaking POV

She picked up her POV immediately

Now you know what POV is. You're not head-hopping? Or are you? Let's go through all the little ways that you can break this uranium-plated law.

So to the first rule: establish POV as soon as possible. For first and second that's pretty easy, you just have a sentence with 'I' or 'you' in it. For third limited, it's harder. In practical terms it means that one of the first sentences of a section should be in the POV of the focus character. I say 'one of': you're fine sticking some omniscient description in there, but the first sentence dealing with a sentient being should be to do with your point of view character.

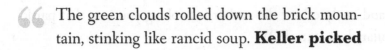 The green clouds rolled down the brick moun-
tain, stinking like rancid soup. **Keller picked**

up his pogo stick, grimaced, and adjusted the fusion drive. It was go time.

Here's a pretty standard section start. I've established the setting, and then established the POV character. *It was go time* is one of those weird little sentences you see all the time in fiction: it's not quite in POV but it's not quite out of it. It might be the narrator or the character thinking it, but it doesn't matter. Okay, here's the next paragraph.

> I hope we can make it to the nest in time, **Mabel thought**.

Wha-wha-wha-whaaaat? Why is Mabel thinking when we're in Keller's POV? It's because I broke the rule. It turns out, I was using Keller as a descriptive element, and I threw my reader out when they read it. (Yeah, and I just unreliable narratored you, how do you like them apples?)

It's easy to fix though. Just put some little action for Mabel to do, right from the get go.

> The green clouds rolled down the brick mountain, stinking like rancid soup. **Mabel strolled through the camp**, mug in hand. She waved at Keller. He nodded back, picked up his pogo stick, and grimaced while adjusting the fusion drive. It was go time.

Easy. Get your POV character doing something as soon

as possible. By the way, I've seen an argument that this is one of the few times that filtering is desirable. If your character is really doing nothing and so you can't easily write them an action, then having them watch the beige sun rising above the dirty fog might be acceptable if it's establishing their POV.

I didn't mean to be in your head

The next is more subtle. It's when you get in someone's head by accident.

> The nuclear pogo stick whined and thudded as Mabel bounced up the artificial cliff, the rest of the team not far behind. Keller kept up a constant patter of obscenities over the com, **terrified of** the great drop below him. A nesting flock of jubjub birds gazed at the foolish human interlopers **smugly**, their pink feathers shivering in the breeze.

Can you see it? That's right: I broke POV twice. We're not in either Keller or the jubjub bird's heads so we can't tell if they are terrified or smug. This isn't a big head-hop: you don't get that whiplash like you did earlier. However, you're still breaking your reader's trust by pulling them, shallowly, into too many directions.

Yeah, that's kind of sad, isn't it? The tension of the situation partly derives from the interaction between the characters. As a result, it's the sort of sentence that, unlike some of the other things we wrote, we'll really miss if we cut it. I even used an adverb-as-art because birds can't look smug and man I'll be sore to lose that.

The first cure might be worse than the disease, and that's to use the most weaselly of weasel words: *obviously* (along with its cousins such as *clearly* and *plainly*). Yes it's an adverb, and a nasty one too. But it absolutely gets us out of our predicament.

> Keller kept up a constant patter of obscenities over the com, **obviously** terrified of the great drop below him.

Ew. And yet I have seen this done by best-selling authors who have sold enough books that if they wanted to, they could bury me in donated copies. So, I guess that makes it okay?

It's worth analysing why this works, before we move on. What I'm using is a very clever little get out. Yes, I'm not in his head, but the narrator and Mabel can obviously see that he's obviously terrified because it's so obvious with all the obvious things that he's obviously doing, so it's Mabel's experience, and it's not head hopping okay?

And then it's worth analysing why this is bad: because I am absolutely telling not showing.

But. Friends. *Obviously* is an adverb (*Stephen King will obviously eat it*), and we have a rack of buzzsaws over there, in a box labelled 'fixes for adverbs.' So let's roll that out and root around in it, shall we?

If we were revising and we found *obviously* and we were thinking about it as an adverb, we wouldn't just delete it without thinking about it. (Well, we would sometimes, but that gets us back to where we started, which isn't much help, so let's instead look deeper.) Remember the golden rule with adverbs. What weakness is it propping up? And in this case, it's weak direct speech. What weak direct speech is that, I hear you ask? Yeah, exactly. There is none. We'd summarized it and hadn't realised it, so let's actually show it and put it in.

> 'Oh, for all the frakks in the sky, we're a long way up...' Keller muttered over the open com channel.

So there's a better cure for POV breakage. Instead of saying what's going on in their head, show it, through dialogue or action. And if you can't... Ask yourself: how your narrator could know?

There are less weaselly words than *obviously*.

> Keller kept up a constant patter of obscenities over the com. **He looked** terrified of the great drop below him.

This is using a different structure. Here we know exactly how Mabel can tell he is terrified: he looks it. This is also fine, but, honestly, I prefer the deep immersion of the direct speech.

For the birds, I think I would change it to this:

> A nesting flock of jubjub birds gazed at them, their feathers shivering in the breeze.
> Smug pink bastards, Mabel thought.

Again, we're unambiguously in her head.

Summary

Point of view is hard. To avoid ambiguity, establish it as early as possible in every new section with little actions from your POV character.

Check for micro-POV breaks involving thoughts leaking from other characters' heads. To fix these you have two options. Use a weasel word like *obviously,* although generally try not to do this. Or, better, write out what they are doing from the POV character's actual point of view. This can be quite deep, where you write their impressions as thoughts or actions; or it can be shallow where you use words like *looked like* to indicate why the POV character knows what's going on.

Chapter 13

I echoed echoed echoed and then reverberated

Duped by duplicates

We're leaving a deeply technical chapter, and moving on to something very simple. It's time to talk about repetition of words, sometimes called 'echoing.' The concept is very simple: don't reuse the same word.

> The demonic flan was heavy in my **hands**, the cursed pastry quivering with rage. I knew what it wanted: to fly from my **hands** and destroy my enemies. It whispered eldritch curses and writhed in my **hands**.

Can you see it? Of course, you can. I repeated a lot of words. But the one that sticks out is *hands*. I mean it partly sticks out because I bolded them, but even without that, it's really obvious.

So what's the problem? It's just... clunky. When we read, some aspect of the pleasure we get is almost like when we're watching the rain or a fire: we see lots of micro variation that combines to make an emergent structure. Repetition of words messes with us because it ruins that sentence-level variety.

The other problem is, of course, that our reader might think that we're accidentally repeating ideas. I have this motif of holding the flan, and I keep banging on about it.

Let's fix it.

> The demonic flan was heavy in my **hands**, the cursed pastry quivering with rage. I knew what it wanted: to fly from my **grip** and destroy my enemies. It whispered eldritch curses and writhed.

I changed the second *hands* to *grip*. I simply deleted the third.

It's interesting, because when we talk about echoing we don't just mean any old words. No! For example, you can crank out conjunctions and pronouns until the possessed pastries come home and no one will care (although remember our new friend the polysyndeton from the run-ons chapter). No, it's the big four that we care about: nouns, verbs, adjectives and adverbs. *Hands* is a noun, we've seen that. Let's look at some of the others echo.

> I'd had the flan for nearly six months. I'd **baked** it on New Year's Day, just as a bet. A

friend had told me that if I'd never **baked** a flan before, that was the day to do it.

So I **carefully** bought all the ingredients and **carefully** followed the recipe. It was **easy**, if I'm going to be honest. Given how **easy** it was, I should have realised the danger I was in.

Lotta repetition there. It's almost like I wrote that passage to show it, isn't it?

Although, look a bit more closely. There's a lot of repetition of words other than the verb *baked*, the adverb *carefully* and the adjective *easy*. I use the word *I* a lot. But pronouns don't suffer from the same echo penalty as the big four. In fact, a common short word will echo much less. However, if you really hammer them, you'll see them.

> **I** was dumbfounded. What was **I** going to do? **I** was alone. **I** was afraid. **I** was stuck in a house with baked goods from hell.

It's almost like different words have different echo values. The heavyweight ones are the rare ones, and they really stick out when you repeat them. The more common they are, the more you can use them. Which is lucky, really: imagine if you had to worry about echoing on *the*.

Because of that, when you do see echoing on a short, common word, you don't have to prune as fiercely.

> What was **I** going to do? **I** was alone, and afraid... And **I** was stuck in a house with baked goods from hell.

Three *I*s seems about right. The unsatisfying first sentence just got axed, and I realised that the list of *I was* meant I could put them into a list.

Look, this is the line editing technique that everyone knows. So, we're done, right?

Not so fast.

But but but I wanted the echo

But maybe you want to repeat yourself for dramatic effect. And if you do, the simple guideline is for it to be purposeful.

> I wanted to make peace with the flan. I **tried,** I **tried,** I **tried.** My friends assumed the padlock on my fridge was to keep me out, not it in. I begged at it through the door as it thrashed around in the crisper, pulping my cucumber and shredding my lettuce. I **tried**, so very hard, but in the end... I gave up.

Here I'm using repetition for emphasis: it's the focus of this paragraph. I think this works better in first or deep third than in limited third, because I reckon the way that a first-person narrator tells a tale is more amenable to quirks of speech such as this. But that's just me; you can make it work everywhere. The idea, though, is to go all-in. Use the repeti-

129

tion decisively and for impact, and like anything, use it sparingly, or your text will read like a picture book.

But this, ah, you knew all this. You didn't need to read my book for this!

What do you call a dinosaur which knows what words mean?

So to add a tiny bit of value, I'm going to talk about a thing that I think writers do to avoid echoing, and can be just as bad: to use uncommon words.

It's so easy to pull up a thesaurus – I have one on my computer, right now, I'm sure you do too – and look for synonyms to get yourself out of your echo trouble. You are a writer, a wordsmith, a lover of speech and the magic you can perform with it... So let's perambulate to the metronomic cadence, and disgorge some iridescent articulations!

Woah there. Woah woah woah.

I'm sure you know what all those words mean, but your reader might not. So the question is, should you keep them? Is it better to vocabularize our way out of an echo than delete it?

The truth is, it's not clear. You should consider your audience's age and sophistication, and the pace of the story at that point. It's really hard though: when I researched for this piece, I found someone complaining about the use of the word *ostentatious* which I don't consider all that, well, ostentatious. Putting myself into the shoes of a reader doesn't mean I'll know what words they know.

I think the best solution is the easiest. Find a few books which you consider to be at the level you are writing for.

Read them, and keep an eye out for the big words. Look for how frequently they're being dropped in, and whether they're used in action or slower sections. This is good advice generally, by the way: it will help you be guided on other things too, like how much horror, sex, violence and pudding exorcists are appropriate in your work.

But don't sweat it too hard. You can't know everyone's vocabulary level, and if your reader is enjoying it, they'll forgive you for having to look up the odd word, and some people enjoy having their vocabulary expanded this way. A longer word that really punches hard can be something that will improve your text with little cost.

One last note: if you're worried about this, when you introduce an important technical term, you can explain what it means. This works particularly well for nouns. Not everyone knows what *hauberk, embolism, albumen,* or *marmalade* means. Well, they might know that last one.

Now this is a pretty heavy-handed technique: if you're going to do it, it had better be an important thing. No one likes this done as lazy world-building in science fiction and fantasy. You're just wasting people's time when you do that. But assuming that this is actually Chekhov's marmalade, let's go.

You can explain it quickly inline.

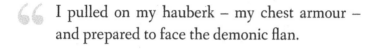

> I pulled on my hauberk – my chest armour – and prepared to face the demonic flan.

You can use dialogue.

> 'Hahaha! You can't eat me! My bedevilled trans fats will give you an embolism,' shrieked the possessed pudding.
>
> 'Thanks!' I replied. 'That'll look lovely in my living room.'
>
> 'You moron, an embolism is a blocked artery!'

Or you can just take a detour and exposition it there and then.

> I reviewed my pastry recipe, going through the glossary carefully. Albumen is the science name for the egg white. I knew this. But I'd skimmed over the bit that said that one in twenty eggs bought at the end of December are cursed, and can only be used safely in omelettes or break-fasts. No wonder no one else eats flan on New Year's Day!

Summary

Look out for echoes.

To fix, swap another word in. Be careful that you don't put in words that alienate your readers. To find out if they do, read at the level you're writing for, although don't obsess, because there is leeway here.

However, for technical terms, you can explain them, and if they are important, maybe you should, although don't use this as a lazy world-building substitute.

Chapter 14

'Use speech tags properly,' she ululated

Tagging and bagging

Broadly you can slice your story into three bits: dialogue, narration, and action. Or something? Maybe exposition is separate? You can find people who will argue about that and re-slice it for you. I'm not going to fight with you, everything you've written is amazing.

We've mentioned direct speech often, we've skirted around some of the issues, now it's time to pull the conch shell from the death god's hands, and pour the river of blood over our heads while screaming the unholy rite of the end, like we do every weekend. Right? Right? Right? Oh no. Don't tell anyone.

Moving on. Dialogue has very, very different rules to the rest of what we write. It's different because it's subjective and yet you don't need to worry about showing rather than telling. When your characters say something, they do so from their own point of view, not the narrator's. The distance you can put between your character's voices and your narrator's voice is important to establish their independence and their individual personalities. But that's not interesting, because we aren't talking about the whole world of writing, we're interested in the craft of line editing. I'm sure you figured out your characters ages ago.

As you've probably noticed, for the things that are said by your characters, you can ignore pretty much this entire book so far. Adverbs: use 'em! Adjectives: whatever you feel like! You're reporting your character's stumbling confessions, and they say all that stuff. Fragments, as we said, are to be used carefully. Echoing is harder, and you need to make sure you only do it consciously, because your reader will notice it, even through inverted commas, despite the fact that humans echo all the time. So even when your baked goods are screaming at each other, don't repeat the word *hands*, okay?

But the thing that we're going to spend the majority of time on this chapter isn't what your beloved characters are saying: it's how you know who's saying what. Yes, it's speech tags. It's the little dollops of text between spoken dialogue.

This is a great big grab bag of rules and guidelines, some enforced harder than others, so we're going to just blunder through it all and see what we get.

Rule One – action beats

An action beat is a bit of text in speech which signals who's speaking, without explicitly saying *said* or equivalent. Used judiciously, they can enhance your dialogue because they break up the rhythm.

The two of them crouched in the control room.

'You don't understand.' **Cressida pulled the motherboard from her backpack.** 'I had it. I had it all along. It doesn't matter what Kronos does.'

Malcolm shook his head. 'That doesn't make any sense. It was in the Omnivore's power assembly.'

Cressida smiled, and the sun caught her space teeth. They glittered like the end of the world.

'Yes, it was. And then I taught the Omnivore about gymkhana. It loves the tiny ponies. We're going to be okay, Malcolm. We're going to be okay.'

Action beats are good because they move the story on and remove repetition and also give us flavour. Absolute win-win. However, overuse makes your characters twitchy; mundane action beats make it boring. If you're very unsure, start with 50/50 action beats to regular speech tags.

These are related to stage directions, too. We'll look at them in chapter sixteen.

Rule Two – Don't be afraid of said

Don't be afraid of *said*. Yes it's a verb, but it's a special one because it's pretty much invisible. You need to use it a lot to get it to echo, so sprinkle it around fairly liberally. It's tempting to use more complicated speech tag verbs, but they get gloopy at best and make your readers hate you at worst (see rule nine).

> 'You have nothing,' Kronos **said**. 'It's over. In ten days I'll be in every calculator in Belgium. They'll all just print out 8008135 and that thing where it says "Shell Oil" when you turn it upside down. And the can-can. You can do nothing, puny human.'
>
> Cressida picked up the Omnivore's motherboard, and the light shone in her space hair. It sparkled like a supernova.
>
> 'You might think that,' she **said**. 'But look what I have here...'

I used two *saids*, and I bet you didn't notice, right?

Rule Three – Use asked, answered, and their friends correctly

Use *asked* when someone asks a question. Never pair a question with a *said* or a statement with an *asked*. You can use *replied* when someone, you know, replies. There are a few other, similar, neutral speech tags which can be used in a similar way without going over the top: for example, *observed, remarked, agreed*. But, unlike *said*, these will trigger echoing more easily, so treat them carefully.

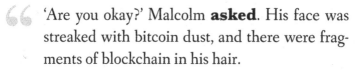 'Are you okay?' Malcolm **asked**. His face was streaked with bitcoin dust, and there were fragments of blockchain in his hair.

'I've been better,' Cressida **replied**. Her space eyes gleamed in the darkness. 'But I'm intact. How are you?'

Malcolm stood up. As he rose, the half-built consensus fell to pieces around him, collapsing into shards that skittered across the metal floor.

'I'm basically fine. Listen, Cressida. I... Maybe...? Oh dammit. Will you marry me?'

Rule Four – Very few adverbs

As we said already, avoid adverbs on speech tags unless – maybe – they indicate speech directions that we have no way of showing in the speech. But always strive to use dialogue which shows your intent, rather than adverbs.

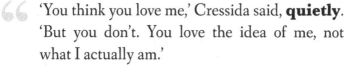 'You think you love me,' Cressida said, **quietly**. 'But you don't. You love the idea of me, not what I actually am.'

The tears in her eyes sparkled like distant stars.

'I'm not human enough for you,' she continued. 'I'm made of the same stuff as the void. This, all this, it's your world. You're lovely, Malcolm, you really are. But I need to return to my original form, and if you were with me, that would destroy you.' She pushed back a lock of

hair, and smiled, despite it all. 'I'll miss the shuf-
fleboard, too.'

That has one borderline adverb and I actually think I'd
nix it, because it's got the pathos of a lovestruck baby
elephant loose in a glass-blowers. You can convey so much
emotion with little actions and careful speech, so really dial
the *ly* words back, probably remove them.

Rule Five – Cressida said

In today's world it's *Cressida said*, not *said Cressida*. This
rule works for all fiction, including works that don't include
Cressida. It's supposedly less stuffy, and symmetrical with
other tag use (*I said, she said*). Again: if you're interested, dig
around in your books, and look for recent stuff. When I did, I
found the same results as I did for semicolons in speech: it's a
modern development, from the US, and it's definitely a
thing.

Rule Six – Use your mouth

Use speech verbs which actually describe making words
with your mouth.

> 'I will destroy you,' Kronos **gloated**.
> 'No you won't,' Malcom **laughed** back.

You can say something gloatingly, and you can laugh
after you say something, but you can't gloat something or

laugh something. They are both verbs but they don't actually describe the act of making noises with your fleshy meat-sack mouth. This feels like a kicker, until you realise that you're really being helped with showing rather than telling. *Gloatingly* is absolutely in the domain of adverbs and I don't need it, I should strengthen my speech. If I make my laughter an action beat, it will make it better.

> 'I will crush you. I will destroy you and I won't even notice your absence. You will be nothing but vile organic stains on my metal floors,' said Kronos.
>
> 'No you won't.' Malcolm stared into the camera **and laughed**.

It's still weird because it sounds so unnatural that he stopped and chuckled, but this is equivalent to what we wrote before and highlights why *laughed* is such a weird speech tag. You don't tend to laugh when you speak, you laugh in response to something else, so using it to indicate what people say is actually not a very natural thing.

Having said that, this one is probably the weakest of all the rules. You sometimes see published authors doing this (my bugbear is *snorted*. I have absolutely seen that used as a speech tag in a novel, and I hate it. Reader challenge: right now, snort some speech. Yeah, exactly) so if you wanna do it, do it, but be aware that it's weakening your text just ever so slightly.

Rule Seven – Vary the position of tags

Vary the position of tags.

> 'Oh Malcolm, I'm so glad to see you,' **Lotty said**.
>
> **Malcolm slumped into the front seat of the Fiat Currency**. 'She's gone, Lotty. Gone forever.' Rain streaked the windscreen, clearing paths in the crypto dust.
>
> 'I know she meant a lot to you.' **Lotty didn't start the engine**. Instead, she just stared at her key fob, a tiny model of a spleen. 'I know, also, that you liked her a lot. But Malcolm – this day always had to come.'

I put tags at the beginning, the middle and the end. Only one is a tag, the others are action beats. Tags at the front are quite old fashioned, and people tend to only use action beats there. Be careful with tags at the end, though. You can confuse your readers with particularly long speeches that end with a tag; what if they think that it's someone else speaking and then realise at the end? Do they reread the whole section? I think for short bits of dialogue it's probably okay, though.

The other thing about that previous section is that I arguably overused them. So...

Rule Eight – You can drop them

You can drop the tags completely if it's unambiguous as to who's talking, particularly if there are two people and one of them uses the other one's name.

> 'Lotty, thanks so much for what you said earlier,' said Malcolm. 'It really helped.'
>
> 'You're welcome, Malcolm. I know I don't have space feet like Cressida did, but I... I can do cool stuff too.'
>
> 'You do the coolest stuff, Lotty. You do the coolest stuff.'
>
> She smiled, turned, and walked away. Then, with a kick as swift as a comet, she scored the winning penalty in the World Cup final.
>
> The crowd erupted around them.

Here's a rule of thumb: when you have only two people in the scene, you should limit the speech without tags to four bits of dialogue.

> The cold wind rattled around them, and they snuggled closer. Malcolm blew the steam from his hot chocolate, and then pulled a shard of plastic from his pocket. It was burnt, and stained, and looked like nothing at all.
>
> 'I found this.'
>
> 'What is it?'
>
> 'It's a bit of the Omnivore's casing. It must

> have fallen off when we... When Cressida and I
> fought Kronos.'
>> 'It was a year ago, wasn't it? I'm sorry,
> Malcolm.'
>> Malcolm kissed Lotty's forehead. A
> shooting star raced across the sky.
>> 'It doesn't matter,' **he said**. 'I'm happy. I
> hope you are, too.'

Yeah, it's about right, isn't it? When I reread it, I was tempted to put an action beat on Lotty's remark about it being a year ago, mostly for pacing, but it works without, too. We're trying not to get in the way of our dialogue: at the end of the day, we want to immerse our readers.

Rule Nine – No gloopy tags

This is the most important rule here. Beware of tags which draw too much attention to themselves. Use them sparingly, not as a universal solution to reduce your *said* echo.

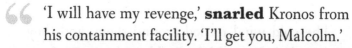

> 'I will have my revenge,' **snarled** Kronos from
> his containment facility. 'I'll get you, Malcolm.'
>> 'Boss, I have the codes to every vending
> machine in Omaha,' **stuttered** a binary under-
> ling. 'Will that help?'
>> 'It's not enough,' **growled** Kronos. 'I need
> more.'
>> 'How about access to all the game consoles
> in... the world?' **sneered** Ouroboros.

A digital grin crept across Kronos' visual display cortex.

'That is an excellent place to start,' he **gloated**. 'An excellent place...'

These definitely need dialling down. Really heavy speech tags make your speech feel overwrought and amateurish, and test your reader's patience (and drive professionals up the wall). The one I hate the most here is *sneered*. People don't actually sneer that much in real life, and so it sounds cartoony.

Even relatively neutral non-*said* tags can do this, so be very careful on trying to inject interest by varying the tags. The right place to put the interest is your sparkling dialogue itself.

Summary

Speech tags are complicated! Here are the nine rules.

1. Use action beats, but not too often. Start with 50/50 action beats to speech tags.

2. Don't be afraid of *said*.

3. Use *asked, answered* and *replied* appropriately: other context-specific neutral tags are good too. Beware of echo.

4. Avoid adverbs: the only ones you use should disambiguate your speech or be absolute hydrogen bombs of brilliance.

5. *Cressida said* is cool these days, *said Cressida* is not.

6. Use speech verbs which involve actual reality-based talking: for example, people don't actually *laugh* or *snort* speech. However, published writers break this one, so.

7. Vary the position of tags. In modern fiction, initial tags tend to be action beats. Be careful with tags at the end of a long speech.

8. You can drop the tags completely if it's unambiguous as to who's talking, and having speech use names is good for that. In a scene with two people, a good rule of thumb is four pieces of dialogue without tags.

9. Be wary of too many strong tags; it's the speech of the characters we want to lift, not the tags. If you only observe one rule, this is the one to keep.

Further reading

The Scribophile article on speech tags is fantastic. It goes into loads of detail, and also talks about punctuation things like em-dashes and commas which I totally ignored, because, man, punctuation!?... https://www.scribophile.com/acad emy/he-said-she-said-dialog-tags-and-using-them-effectively

Yes, of course I'm going to cite Louise Harnby. I promise I'm not on her payroll. The thing I like about this article is how she talks about double-telling as a way of hunting for breaks of our precious rule nine. https://www.louiseharn byproofreader.com/blog/dialogue-tags-and-how-to-use-them-in-fiction-writing

Chapter 15

I felt that I had probably lost descriptive certainty

How big is your hedge?

This one is fun. It's about being completely confident in your writing, and erasing what I'm calling your 'descriptive uncertainty.' I say 'what I'm calling' because there's a class of similar problems which don't seem to have a name, so I gave it one; and some of the types of those problems are also unnamed, so I gave them names too. I'm probably wrong, and you can laugh at me when you find what they're actually called.

Let's start with the easiest, which does have a name, and that's hedging.

> The garden was **about** the size of a football pitch.

Hedge words... are to do with well-manicured gardens, right? Yes! No. They're so-called because they're about hedging your bets. When you use a hedge word, you aren't committing fully to your narrative, and you get wishy-washy with your descriptions.

By the way, the above example is from my in-progress SF horticulture novel, *Topiary of Tomorrow*, which features both types of hedging.

Here I'm waving my hands about the size of the garden. I could just come out and say that it's the size of a football pitch. No one is going to get out a tape and measure it.

> The garden was the size of a football pitch.

But I think there's a deeper truth than this.

I claim that we hedge because we're mixing our narrator's voice with our character's voice. My POV character, Ensign Sunil, isn't waving a tricorder round, which means he has no idea how big it is. He might glance around, guess that the place was about the size of a football pitch, and not be interested enough to form a solid opinion. Like if you held a phaser to his head and screamed, 'Sunil how big is the damn garden?' he'd be all 'Dude who are you? Where did you come from? How do you know my name? I don't know! Leave me alone!'

But we know. We as the writer have a good idea, and we want to tell our reader. So, we end up in this compromise, in this semi-omniscient-but-also-limited-yeah-I'm-not-picking-a-side mode. Or sometimes we don't know, but we want to sorta wave that fact away and keep going.

And we hedge our bets. And we get hedging words.

Well, I'm here to tell you: pick a darn side. You're either describing in omniscient, in which case you know its every dimension and what every plant is and where the gardener keeps the robo-trowels, in which case you should be very confident in the size... Or you're in limited in which case your experience is the colours and smells and how the alien bugs buzz around and the birds scream at each other. If you commit to one of the two, you can avoid hedging.

Back to my novel. Sunil is imprisoned in an alien dome, which contains a replica of a famous space federation garden.

> It looked **a bit like** the original on Earth, but instead of a croquet lawn, it had **a variety of** trees.

A bit like is more of the same, and the problem here is how wishy-washy that line is. It's fine to say something is like something else, we do that all the time with similes; but if we're comparing a specific thing to another specific thing, then we need to be quite specific, and when we use *a bit* we're trying to sweep that specificity under the carpet. If there are differences or similarities, we should clearly say what they are. In the example above, I don't.

I say it's a bit like the original, you know? No, you say. I do not know. It could be a bit like a garden where it's the same but all the air has been replaced with gorgonzola cheese, you say, that's a bit like the original.

So what do we do? Be more explicit! Stop hedging.

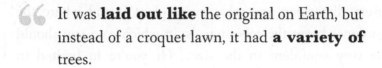

> It was **laid out like** the original on Earth, but
> instead of a croquet lawn, it had **a variety of**
> trees.

Better? Yeah. Best? Nope!

What are *a variety of trees*? What they are, my good
reader friend, is a total shirking of my responsibilities as a
writer. But, yes, I know, researching trees is hard! It's the
kind of thing that can take you down a rabbit hole for an
evening. Which if I'm going to be completely honest, I'd be
fine with because I'm a massive nerd, but not much writing
would get done.

So, back onto my original hobby horse. I think that I'm in
this mess because I'm skirting on the edge of omniscient
mode. This is a thing which happens in descriptive passages.
And I keep hedging because it requires me to understand,
well, everything. Which means as soon as I try to describe
space gardens, not being a gardener from space, I'm lost.

Looking at my manuscript, I have an entire paragraph of
this stuff. Maybe I should reset. I think I'll try again from the
beginning.

> The garden took Sunil's breath away. The
> croquet lawn and summer house he recognised,
> but everything else was new. The lawn was
> surrounded by unfamiliar trees: they looked like
> willows, although their long trailing leaves were
> pink, and covered in tiny grey flowers. The air
> was heavy with the scent of thyme. The foun-
> tain had been replaced with a sculpture made

of floating silver cubes, which shimmered in the still air.

I remember that fountain, he thought. My parents took a photo of me, standing right here, when I graduated from the academy.

But not really here. I've never been here before.

He looked up, and stared at the grey dome.

I hope Isidora is on her way.

I took a step back and tried to make it explicitly from Sunil's POV. Did I succeed? Maybe. Maybe not. I focused on micro details rather than macro, and that meant I was able to give you concrete things which Sunil experienced.

It's worth saying at this point that hedging isn't always bad in writing. Scientific papers are many hedges for every presented fact. That's because you can't just say that eating cars kill you: you have to say that in the studies conducted most accidental deaths involving the consumption of vehicles appeared to indicate a positive correlation within statistical significance. I hedge constantly in this book, because really there's no right answers and plus I don't want to look like a dick who's ordering you around and that softens it a bit. But hedging in fiction isn't great.

The horror I saw was beyond my ability to describe

Here's another type of descriptive uncertainty. What do you think of this?

> The bird hopped down to Sunil's feet and made
> an indescribable noise.

This isn't hedging. This is flat out saying, nope, no way I know anything about this, so I'm not writing it at all! I've totally committed, but I went the wrong way. The cosmic horror writers were a big fan of this technique. It kind of stinks because it's just not bothering to paint a picture.

I don't know what this is called, so I'm calling it descriptive collapse.

Again, I think we get this because we mix our narrator's and our character's voices. Sunil may have never heard anything like the territorial call of a lesser-throated sand gurner, and I'm trying to express that, but the writing style looks like a detached omniscient narrator's voice which gives the impression that I'd given up.

So how to fix? You zoom in closer, or you pull out further. Here's where go in:

> The bird hopped down to Sunil's feet. I hope to
> hell that thing's not venomous, he thought.
>
> It screamed at him, and he jumped back in
> surprise. He'd heard nothing like that before,
> ever, and it chilled his blood. His hand dropped
> to his phaser.

I tried to go more into Sunil's head. This is still a fairly distant limited third, but I've used the POV to explain that he's never heard the sound before. I didn't describe the call but I also didn't lose descriptive certainty.

Here's where, instead of going into Sunil's head, I pull out:

> The bird hopped down to Sunil's feet. It cocked its head to one side and then made a noise like a pinball machine exploding in a meat locker, all staccato metal rattles on wet flesh.
> Sunil jumped back, alarmed.

Sunil is an ensign on the USS Secateurs, and in his future world they don't eat sausages or play pinball. But it doesn't matter, because I described the thing from my omniscient position, for you, oh Earthling, who does know what both of those things are. Although, to be fair, I haven't seen a pinball machine for ages, so maybe that's no good.

This is a thing that a certain kind of comic writer does a lot. Douglas Adams and Terry Pratchett constantly broke POV from limited third into omniscient to make jokes about their worlds. They always had narrative certainty because they never shied away from panning the camera right out to show a 'meanwhile, over here' gag if something was going to be difficult to explain, and often that's where their best stuff comes from.

This arguably only works in comedy. And, if you're doing it, it needs to be established that this is your style early on, otherwise it's super weird if it happens half way through the book for the first time.

Engage hyper filtering!

The third and final piece of descriptive uncertainty also doesn't have a name that I could find. I'm calling it hyper filtering.

> He was finally going to go home.
> Sunil **felt** a smile creep onto his face. He **realised** that he was holding his turbo hedge-trimmer.

You remember filtering? We were all so young and innocent back then, weren't we? If you don't, that's when we unnecessarily filter our reader's experience through our character's senses. If you still don't, you could go back and reread chapter two?

We have filtering there – *felt* and *realised*. But looking beyond the filtering, this is kind of strange. It heavily implies that poor old Sunil doesn't have full control of his body and mind. Now, if he's been stung by a green-leaved fly chewer and the neurotoxin has just kicked in, well, fair enough. That's a reason to keep filtering words, because, as you remember, if it's important that we know what a character is experiencing, that's not filtering.

However, let's be honest. We sometimes use this sort of phrase because we don't really want to commit to an emotional state or action: as a result our characters suddenly find themselves doing things. We've abandoned descriptive certainty about their motives.

I think I'd rewrite as follows.

> He was finally going to go home.
> Sunil couldn't suppress his smile. The turbo hedge trimmer thrummed in his hands, forgotten in his delight.

Much nicer.

But... I've seen hyper filtering in successful published fiction! So for this one you can wave paperbacks at me and tell me I'm a moron. Although please don't do that if, say, I'm at a funeral. Have some respect, damn it.

What about this?

> The cold crept up his right arm, as the poison seeped through his veins. He looked down and **realised** that he was clicking his fingers.
> Oh no.
> He staggered, retching.
> He was singing... He knew that. Old songs. Putting on his top hat...
> The grass came up to meet his face, spores lazily dancing in his vision.
> **He felt** his feet tapping, possessed of a life of their own. They drummed in a rhythm on the turf. He had no idea what his tails where, or why he was brushing them off. He was moving his whole body now, hitting a beat that he didn't understand, his life possessed by the music...

Your response to this passage will probably be what the heck is going on here?

I'm using hyper filtering to try and create the strange, toxin-induced state which poor Sunil is experiencing. But it's completely incomprehensible. I mean, it doesn't help that I'm referring to a song that was written before even I was born: but even without that the imagery is super vague, and finally I pour the kerosene of hyper filtering onto the dumpster fire.

This is about balancing your desire to show your character's confusion with your need to concretely tell your reader what's going on. If you go too far in that particular direction it's no fun for anyone. So be careful with hyper filtering even when there is neurotoxin involved.

Summary

Descriptive (un)certainty! Don't look it up, I made it up.

Hedging: *a bit, about, sort of, probably, some kind of, just, must be, could, might, maybe, some, a little, almost...* either delete the word or commit.

Descriptive collapse: *indescribable, impossible to describe, unreadable expression* and so on. Either go in, so describe it from your character's POV, in which case you can directly reflect your character's confusion; or go out, in which case you can describe it using things your character has no familiarity with.

Hyper filtering: like filtering but turned up to eleven. Why has your character lost control of their faculties? Is it important or are you being unclear? Either way, fix by being certain.

Further reading and listening

It's surprisingly hard to find pieces to read about hedging in fiction. Most of the stuff you'll see in a search is on hedging in academic papers, or other, unrelated sorts of hedging. This is quite good because it has a list of the words to look out for. Note that some of them are also (shudder) adverbs. https:// theeditorsblog.net/2010/11/18/hedge-words/

The reliably funny 372 *Pages We'll Never Get Back* podcast talks about various aspects of descriptive uncertainty, but they give it a different name which is rather rude about a famous SF author.

Chapter 16

He walked and breathed his stage directions

Enter stage left

This is it, we're on the downward slope to the end. It's mostly just little things now, so stick your legs out and freewheel, ringing your bell gleefully! But avoid the crocodile pit.

This one's about what's known in the trade as 'stage directions.' These are actions that you describe your characters (and, I guess, props) making. They don't tend to be terribly interesting, and so when you're editing you need to decide how much they're propelling the story forwards. However, if you have too few, your reader doesn't know where your characters are or what they're doing. So, the magic here is deciding what to cut and what to keep.

Here's an example of some dialogue mixed in with stage directions. Look at all the movement.

> **Ariane stepped towards the portal**, drawn by her curiosity and its strange gravity.

She lifted her hand up and had to fight hard to stop it from being sucked in.

'That's weird,' she said. **She turned to Gregor**. 'So if I go through there I'll end up in a magical land full of fauns and elves and stuff?'

Gregor put his hand on her shoulder. 'This one's out of warranty and sends you to a world where you star in cookery shows, so I'd stay away.'

They're called 'stage directions' because they might appear in a script. They tend to be very tied to dialogue. Here's my manuscript continued as an incredibly badly formatted screenplay, to show you what I mean (and if you're reading this on an ebook, it's going to look even worse, apologies for that):

```
Ariane steps back.


            ARIANE

Yeah, I've no desire to be on Iron Chef for
eternity. What else have you got?


            GREGOR
(pointing to a different part of the shop)

Now, over there we have what I call 'The
Lion, the Ring, and the Wizarding' section.
If you'll follow me…
```

```
Gregor walks towards the back of the shop,
followed by Ariane.
```

The three actual stage directions here, where Ariane steps back, Gregor points, and they both walk are the kind of thing we're talking about. Although this kind of description might be necessary in scripts so you can block out character movement (maybe? I know exactly nothing about screen writing) they tend to bog down fiction and so we have to treat them with caution. But they're also vital for some writing: after all, action scenes are very heavy with stage directions, and if you don't have enough you can't figure out what's going on. (And by action scenes, I don't just mean when your characters are running away from giant mutant guinea pigs, but this book is very much a PG so we're not going there.)

As a result, unlike, say, hedging, it's one of those things where there's no right answer. It's a stylistic choice, and feeds into the pace of your writing style. There's always going to be someone who doesn't like your pacing, and that's fine. It's why there's room for all of us in this game. But, like all things, understanding what levers we can pull is useful.

Before we start, though, I'm going to briefly moan at you. We call them stage directions, and that maybe makes us think that we're writing for screen. We're not. The difference between visual stories and fiction on the page is passive vs active consumption.

What do I mean by that? Action on the screen is consumed passively. You can enjoy the choreography, the cinematography, the colour palette, and a dozen other things, all without thinking too hard. Now, I'm not intending to belittle cinema or TV: the good stuff gives your mind a workout. However, unlike watchers, readers are forced to consume action actively. This is because most people don't have the ability to hold the physical details of a scene in their mind; they have to work harder to understand what's going on when the bullets are flying. So, you are taxing your reader more for action than for dialogue.

To a lesser degree, this is also true for descriptions, particularly crunchy physical layouts of places and things with lots of distances and angles. I always skip those because I can't visualise them! But action is particularly exhausting if it's done badly, because you can't skim it and still understand the plot. As a result, this is the place where your writing will suffer the most if you don't read enough: you need to get an understanding of both the kind of things that work well on the page, and the way to make them work.

This whole thing could be the subject of an entire book to itself, so I'm not going to go deeper. Instead, I'll focus on the micro, the place we can fix with line editing.

Gotta keep it moving

The best stage directions move the story on in important ways. These are particularly the case in action.

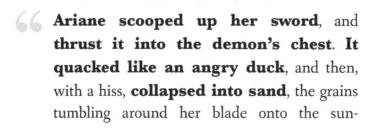

Ariane scooped up her sword, and **thrust it into the demon's chest. It quacked like an angry duck**, and then, with a hiss, **collapsed into sand**, the grains tumbling around her blade onto the sun-bleached earth. **She stepped back**, and **smirked**.

'Yeah, death's a beach, isn't it?' she said.

By my count there are six actions here, plus a dialogue tag. Of them the first four are, I think, essential. She needs to kill the sand demon, and you need to see it dying, otherwise you won't know what happened, so they absolutely stay. The next two, stepping back and smirking, isn't needed. Should I keep them?

And that's where we get into pacing. I like the brief breather before the speech, so I kept those two. You don't have to: they're absolutely not moving the story along which means if I wanted to save a few words, I could delete them.

They showed their inner mood

Stage directions show what characters think without you having to use the dreaded word *obviously*. These tend to be the very things that you don't put into a script, because the actors do it for you.

> Ariane stepped up to the plinth, and put her sword down. Gregor picked up her weapon. He held it briefly, **disdain inscribed on his face**. Then he plunged it into the blade tree, **with far more force than was necessary**.
>
> "'Death's a beach?'" So we do puns now, do

we?' he asked. 'Is it going to be catchphrases next?'

Ariane winced.

'May I remind you,' he continued, **gripping the plinth so hard that his knuckles were white**, 'that we have one rule here, which you are constantly on the verge of breaking. No Eighties movie tropes.'

I used one adverb, *briefly*. Because it's an adverb of time, I claim I can mostly get away with it. However, the intent here was to use stage directions to show what's going through our non-POV character's mind without even slightly breaking POV or using subjective adverbs. Gregor is unhappy, and you know that from his actions, without me writing *Gregor was obviously unhappy*.

For this showing-not-telling emotion thing, you have a lot of tricks. Like, a lot. There's a whole book of them: it's called *The Emotion Thesaurus* and it's entirely full of actions your characters can take to show emotion. You should maybe consider buying it?

But the fact is, you can overuse these. You only need a small number of them. I think I probably went over the top with all the rage symbols.

He breathed cliched stage directions

Yes, show emotion through action and move the plot along, but go easy on the boring and cliched stage directions.

> **Ariane breathed hard** as the rhinos stampeded around them. When they'd finished thundering past, **Gregor walked towards her** with a lazy swagger. **He looked hard at her**, his orange eyes drilling into her soul.
>
> 'I think,' said Ariane, 'that I may have lost a contact lens.'

Your three cliches here are *breathing*, *walking* and *looking*. Every time you see a boring action like this, ask yourself, am I doing this to pad or fill? Can I do it in a better way? Here, Gregor staring at her with a sweaty intensity maybe gets you somewhere later, so fine (but again, this book's a PG); but look, we've all seen the *staring into soul* trope so it might be worth a revision. Walking, though, is really hard to justify in any scene because it's boring, although your reader might be confused by a sudden teleport, so you know, needs must sometimes.

Beware of being too specific with movement. We don't really know where they are in the above example, and it doesn't matter. This is back to my tirade about action being exhausting: all we need to know for this scene is that Gregor is closer to Ariane, not exact distances.

And breathing... Oh, breathing. You are my friend and my enemy. Exhaling, inhaling, holding breaths, they are all cute little action beats because they can carry so much emotion in a little package. It shows inner turmoil by telling of outer struggle. And yet, yes, we can overuse it, and make it cliched for everyone else. It's like some precious natural resource that we have to consume responsibly.

At the end of the day, we want to paint a vivid picture of what's going on. Too few stage directions and too much dialogue and it won't feel rich, the speech will just sit there with no context. Too many action beats, and we're bogged down by people who constantly breathe, walk, look and swallow. They feel fidgety.

In space no one cares about your stage directions

If it's implied you generally don't need to show it.

> Ariane picked up her phone. She found the app, pressed the numbers, and it made a noise that she associated with being underground.
>
> 'We're in a magical alternative realm,' said Gregor. 'I don't think reception's going to be great.'

Yeah you wouldn't write someone using their phone like this. I did it to make a point. But if you think about it, this is a direct command to tell, not show. Yes! We don't show people using the phone, we just tell you that they are. We're breaking the supposed golden rule. But at the end of the day, all stories are telling: there's a reason it's called storytelling, not storyshowing. It's just that through telling we show other things, deeper, implied things. Stage directions are direct statements of what your characters are doing, and you want them to be as pointed as possible, so you don't need to beat around the bush 'showing' people doing mundane things when the reader can understand from context. Just tell your reader that your character tried her phone and omit anything that the reader can easily figure out.

But you'd never write that previous section, right? Okay, so now, let's flip my story to the future. Ariane has gone through a different gate, and is on a space station.

> Ariane sat at the bar. She took her terminal out, and held it up to the interface. She tapped some buttons and transferred enough credits for her drinks into the primary bar account.

This is the same thing as the phone example, but I didn't notice, because I've gotten so deep into my science fiction world building that I've crossed a sort of event horizon of too-much-detail, and I'm being sucked into a black hole of no-one-but-me-cares. I might think I'm building flavour into my world, but, actually, it's just boring. Telling us that she paid is fine. Keep the world building for the interesting stuff.

> Ariane sat at the bar. She paid for her drink at the terminal, and then stared up at the screens.
> Huh. So in the future, sports involve hand puppets, she thought.

Summary

It's the most magical time of the chapter, the summary.

Stage directions are like the bits in a script that aren't scene descriptions or lines. They're not always your friends. Because they are action, they require higher reader engagement.

164

The best ones move the plot along or show emotion, but use a light touch, and think about the rhythm of the prose. If you have too many, your characters twitch. Not enough, and it feels sparse, or your reader doesn't know what's happening.

Ideally, they won't be boring or cliched, and walking and looking fall into this trap. Breathing is useful but borderline.

You can ditch 'obvious' ones and cut to the chase. World building can make you want to write out mundane actions using space words, but actually that slows you down.

Further Reading

Janice Hardy's piece on stage directions is great. She goes deep into a single passage and shows a number of different ways that you can play with them. https://blog.janicehardy.-com/2015/02/finding-right-balance-with-your-stage.html

I mentioned it before, but another shout out: *The Emotion Thesaurus* by Angela Ackerman and Becca Puglisi.

Chapter 17

I vomited gouts of purple prose from my writing implement

Stewed purple words

Have you read *Irene Iddesleigh* by Amanda McKittrick Ros? You should, it's amazing. I found it through the podcast 372 *Pages We'll Never Get Back*. It's very short, you can read it in a couple of evenings, and I did, and I laughed a lot. *Irene Iddesleigh* is one of the worst books ever written, and this is because its prose isn't so much purple, as ultraviolet. It's incredible. It's in the public domain, so you can download a pdf easily.

For this chapter I'm going to show a few different types of excessive writing, or overcooked prose, and we can talk about what to do to fix it.

Before we start, can I show you the drinks menu?

Exclamation! Marks!

The easiest are these! They are exclamation marks! They sound excited! And breathless! And if you use too many they are really irritating! Especially all at once!!!

I think that's quite enough of that.

Generally, you should use them very, very sparingly. The old adage is to have one per book, and that's obviously stupid because it implies that there is some magical threshold which will cause everything to explode if you exceed it: but as a sort of rough rule of thumb I can see why people say that.

I think you should only ever use them in dialogue or thoughts. When a narrative voice is shouting at you, like I was above, it's exhausting. And then, if your characters are shouting at each other all the time, well, that's rather tiring too... But sometimes it makes sense for them to shout because the building is collapsing around them, and it's really noisy. However, maybe they don't need to use exclamation marks to show that unless they are really screaming. You can use *she shouted* speech tags, instead.

Look, this is easy, you get the idea. You don't need me to tell you about this. This was really just an amuse bouche before the starter. Water for the table?

It was very very over-emphasised

With your bouche well and truly amused, let's move onto our appetiser, which is over-emphasis words. Again, these are obvious.

> Leonard picked up the **massive** slice of cheese. It was **extremely** pungent and **hugely** mouldy.
>
> 'Mon dieu,' he said, in his **very** best chef's accent. 'Sacre bleu. Blimey, this stinks...'
>
> He was going to make **truly** the **finest** cheese cake that Luton had ever seen.

Massive, extremely, very, hugely, truly, finest... My writing style gets in the way of the problem here: going over-the-top can be used ironically. If this reads like I'm poking fun at poor old Leonard, well, I want you to know that this is deathly serious because he's making a cheese cake to save Luton from aliens who eat people alive. Yeah, that wiped the smirk from your face, didn't it?

The obvious problem with using superlatives like this is that you run out of road very quickly. If this camembert is extremely pungent, how do I describe the gorgonzola that's been left in a cupboard since 1986?

The less obvious problem is what I call subjectivity. I mentioned it in the adjectives chapter, if you remember. Essentially, when we use words like *massive* we're putting a subjective spin on it: maybe I the writer think it's huge, but you the reader have worked in the brie mines of Wales and thrown away smaller pieces of cheese, and you would be really unimpressed with this puny chunk of fromage.

Then of course *very* is a nasty little word. It's almost always replaceable or removable. It's kind of the opposite of hedging: you're over-adding certainty rather than under-adding it.

So: be careful when you dial up the emphasis. Shall we move on?

Wait, what was that?

No, come on, you can say it.

Really, we're friends now.

You say that I use enormous, gigantic, relentless hyperbole throughout this book and so I'm a colossal, cyclopean, brobdingnagian hypocrite for telling you not to?

Huh.

Yes. Yes, I do use a lot of over-the-top emphasis. And it's nice to talk about it, because it shows how many of the things in this book are just guidelines versus how many are strict rules.

I write my non-fiction with a breathless hyperactive enthusiasm. And I think I mostly get away with it. (Plus I hedge all the time, you noticed that too?) And you're right, this book is in a first person POV, not the detached omniscient POV most textbooks have. So, the accusation you're levelling at me is that I'm writing in a first-person narrative with far, far too many emphasis words, and so I shouldn't be telling you not to.

Is that fair? Maybe. I put a lot of enthusiasm in partly because I'm really enjoying writing this and want to get you excited too... But mostly, because this is dry stuff. We're dealing with technical concepts, gritty parts of grammar that we're taking apart and putting back together again. In contrast, your story won't be boring, so does it need this amount of energy delivered artificially, like added sugar? Or can you let the sweet natural juices of your plot and characters lift its taste? That's why I think you need to be careful with over-emphasis.

Yeah, fine, look at me like that. Let's go to the main course.

Purple reign

I had a go at writing some words that go well beyond over-cooked and ended up burnt to a crisp.

> Leonard's cerulean sight-orbs engorged them-selves on the most perfect of puddings. It sat shimmering like a love-struck humming bird in the autumn rain, seemingly whispering entreat-ments to be gorged upon, to be enjoined with like a fragrant lover. It quivered in anticipation, and Leonard quivered with it, all possible emotions burning through him at once like an exploding star composed of feelings.
>
> He sniffed. 'Yeah, looks alright, I suppose.'

So, first things first, it's surprisingly hard to write really purple prose! It took a lot of editing and thesaurus reading. My word processor doesn't believe me that *entreatments* is a real word, so I definitely reached mauve, at least.

But let's actually analyse this (rather artificial) passage. Purple prose is trying to be poetic but is actually unpleas-antly flowery, and when it's really at maximum violet it's like being assaulted by a roving gang of florists.

What we're looking out for is overly eloquent writing: the sentences are long and complicated, the similes are tortured, and the metaphors are cranked up to eleven in an inappropriate way. And sometimes it's unintentionally hilarious because the writer plucked words from a thesaurus without fully understanding them. It slows the pace and just generally muddies the narrative. Oh, and you spend so much time picking through weird words that you lose interest in the text and the characters, and that is obviously bad.

Now, I'm not here to tell you that poetry can be bad or good, because I know less about writing poetry than I do about quarrying for cheese. But I know this: good poets don't pile on layers of imagery like a crazy wedding cake. What they do is use surprising words judiciously, leave beauty and meaning in the absences between those words, and ensure every word is sharp and simple and chosen to do double or triple duty. So if you want to be poetic in your writing, read good poetry, closely, with a writer's eye. But stay away from anything by Anglo Saxons: they loved alliteration, and if there's one thing that's more purple than a gallon of red grape juice, it's having lots of words all start with the same letter.

One last tip that I will throw in: writing isn't like operating heavy machinery. It's pretty safe to do when drunk or whatever. But when I do write while inebriated, oooh when I read it the next day I wince at what I wrote.

Summary

It's dessert, but let's put aside the profiteroles of pettiness and pick up the pudding spoon of purple prose perspicacity.

Exclamation marks! Use them very little! And probably only in speech or thought.

Be careful with emphasis words, particularly *very* and its

friends, which don't give you much and reduce your available range.

Purple prose is over-flowery language. Its symptoms are tortured sentence construction, over-the-top similes, too many adjectives, over complicated words, and alliteration. The only cure is to rewrite.

Further reading and listening

Reedsy is primarily a marketplace for writing professionals. It's a great place to find, say, an editor. However, they also have a blog, which has some real gems in it. This piece on purple prose goes deep, and has some cracking real-world examples. https://blog.reedsy.com/purple-prose/

372 *Pages We'll Never Get Back* is a book club podcast for bad books. It's very funny, and you only have 158 episodes to catch up. I recommend starting at the start, and as you listen along, you'll learn about some really weird writing quirks to avoid.

Chapter 18

I was using was too much, wasn't I?

Was not

How's it going? It's July here, and the UK has decided that it has had quite enough of this summer nonsense and rain is drizzling down outside, so it's quite pleasant to be sitting in the warm, sipping a cup of tea, writing this.

This chapter is about forms of the verb *to be*. The ways that we normally see this verb are as *was* in past tense, and in present as *is*. In the first paragraph of this chapter, I wrote *is* four times, although most of them are hidden in contractions. We're going to talk about whether those are actually uses of *to be*, whether using them too much is a good thing or not, and what little line edits you can make to clean it up.

Was too many

So why do we want to get rid of *was*? The first is our old friend, echoing. *Was* is a word like any other, and although your tolerance for it is much higher than most other words, it's not infinite. When the *was* really stacks up they can be intrusive. Echoing of *was* is caused by a lot of things, and one of them is the tense you write in. Here's an example.

> Jose **was** afraid. Very afraid. He **was** sure that the thing **was** looking for him, **was** hunting for him through the narrow corridors of the ship: that it **was** worming its slimy bulk through the access ducts. It **was** coming for him, and he **was** afraid.

So, I don't know about you, but I don't notice the repetition of *was* so much as the repetition of *was afraid* at the end. But it's definitely there. And the echoing makes the language feel clunky, not silky.

The reason that we see lots of *was* here is that I'm writing in a tense called the past continuous. Here, *was* isn't actually a use of *to be* in this tense, it's a modifier on another verb which shifts it into the past. And you can't get away from *was* in past continuous. It's how you bolt the words together.

We don't see this tense very often in fiction. Normally we use past simple (*the thing looked for him*) or, sometimes present simple (*the thing looks for him*). The reason I'm using past continuous here is because I'm reporting what Jose thought about in the past. You can tell because of the filter verb *sure*.

If you want to reduce your echoing *was* then this tense is one to avoid. But that's okay! In this case there's a simple fix for that, and it's one we've seen before. Get closer into the character's head!

> Jose shivered in fear. The thing's looking for me, hunting me through the narrow corridors of the ship, he thought. Right now, it's worming its slimy bulk through the access ducts. It's definitely coming for me.

There, much nicer. Less *was*, more intimate. I deleted the last echo, and pushed the rest into reported present continuous. Fascinatingly, contractions solve some of my echo problem: I have a similar number of *is* to *was* but *is* is much more sociable, and wants to be friends with words around it and contracts into stuff like *thing's* and *it's* and provides more variety.

This is interesting. This example is a bit like what we saw with adverbs, where there was a deep fix from a shallow problem. Here, we looked for a problem with echo, and we found out that the solution was re-framing my point of view a little. It's great to think like that, sometimes. Asking yourself whether a scene could do with a shift is a really powerful tool.

For what it's worth, I think past continuous is not as smooth because our language is optimised for the tense that we speak in, which tends to be present simple, and to a lesser degree, past simple. So when you start using weird tenses, it gets a little clunky, just because all the little short cuts aren't there. Those short cuts have been laid down by generations of people making conversation and simplifying common patterns, and you get the benefit of them when you write.

So showing scenes from different views can give you different advantages. It's a good thing to have in your toolkit.

I'm ing ing in the rain

While we're on the subject of past continuous, it's worth saying that generally we like to avoid verbs in their *ing* form. You don't always get a *was* there, so this won't necessarily lower that count, but the general belief is that *ed* forms of verbs are more punchy than *ing* forms.

> The thing **was staring** past him, **gazing** into the darkness beyond. Jose shifted under the broken navigation computer, **remaining** as silent as he could.
>
> It blinked, and then lurched away, off to another part of the ship.

So there are three *ing* verbs here, because there's more past continuous, scattered in the text. However, this time, it's not because of a time shift.

Generally, we should shift to past simple where we can. That's because the continuous tenses are just less punchy than the simple ones. They sound less decisive and you get weird echoing on the *ing*. However, we only do that if it's not going to deteriorate the text too much. There's nothing technically wrong with using this tense, and torturing our sentences unthinkingly by removing all the *ing* verbs will make it worse. I think I'd probably go to this.

> The thing **stared** past him. It **gazed** into the darkness beyond, its pale eyes focussed on some unseen target. Jose shifted under the broken navigation computer, **remaining** as silent as he could.
>
> It blinked, and then lurched away, off to another part of the ship.

The first was an easy switch, from *staring* to *stared*, and *gazing* to *gazed*, but then I found that I disliked the new rhythm. So I broke up the clauses into sentences, and added that last clause to make the sentence feel nice.

The *remaining* I kept. I tried a few possibilities, but didn't like them, and that seemed nice and terse.

I was being too much

Too many *was* can just be an indication that there are too many adjectives. Let's look at an example.

> The hauler **was** a mile from its bow to its stern, a behemoth of metal and plastic orbiting a lonely star. Its AI **was** long dead, its crew departed, its cargo looted. It **was** filled with dust and memories and not much else. It **was** gloomy and forgotten.
>
> Jose's skimmer **was** a beautiful little thing,

fast and graceful. It **was** the closest thing he had to a lover. It **was** barely ticking over as he made a first pass across the great ship.

This is past simple, but even then, I'm definitely using *was* too much, and it echoes more than a reverb unit in a cathedral. All of my sentences are description, and they are stating facts about my world that my reader needs to know. So what do we do here?

Well, these are just adjectives. That's a pretty standard pattern with *to be*, which is *noun was adjective*. For example, *its AI was long dead*. And we know what to do with adjectives!

If you remember, the first thing is to look for the things that are subjective, redundant, or cliches. I don't think anything here is redundant or cliched. But, *gloomy*, *fast*, and *graceful* are arguably subjective, and *beautiful* definitely is. On the other hand, the description of the hauler's size and state are objective. So as a first cut, we could try cleaning up the subjective stuff.

66 The hauler **was** a mile from its bow to its stern, a behemoth of metal and plastic orbiting a lonely star. Its AI **was** dead, its crew departed, its cargo looted. It **was** filled with dust and memories and not much else.

In comparison, Jose's skimmer **was** a tiny dart in the darkness, a bright splinter of energy and speed. It **was** the closest thing he had to a lover. Its engine purred as he made a first pass across the great ship.

Okay, I cleaned all the subjectivity out, even the possible ones. It got a bit flowery, but I think I stayed away from purple. It's somewhat better, but I haven't really pruned my thicket of *was* back much. What next?

The other indication that *was* is telling us is that we're using it as weak verb. *To be* is in some ways the weakest verb of all. If you will indulge me, I will drip some poison in your mind.

Actually, all sentences are *to be* sentences. Everything you write is saying a thing about the world. Even when the thing finds Jose, and it tells him that he has to do his homework and stop messing about with his skimmer, it's a *to be* because I am saying what is, what was. So from that point of view, you never have to use *was* as a verb.

Yes, in some ways, it's like adverbs all over again. *Was* is showing that I could use stronger verbs. Can I improve my example?

> The hauler measured a mile from its bow to its stern, a behemoth of metal and plastic orbiting a lonely star. Scuttled and abandoned a decade ago, it had been looted and stripped to its bones. Now its corridors **were** silent, empty except for dust and memories.
>
> In comparison, Jose's skimmer **was** a tiny dart in the darkness, a bright splinter of energy and speed. He loved it, more than he loved most

people. Its engine purred as he made a first pass across the great ship.

Is it better? I think it is, and that's because by reducing the *was* echo I was forced to use a variety of sentence structures, and they make the text more engaging. They do that not just by reducing the use echo, but also by shifting the rhythms; different orderings, lengths, and intensity of sentences means that I am swept along more easily. Now, I haven't burnt all my *was* away. Two are still there (one hiding as a *were*), and it's fine! They're just words in the crowd now. You don't need to expunge it from your writing completely, and you shouldn't, because you can end up tying yourself into knots.

So. Echoing of *was* might be because you have too many adjectives which need to look at carefully; or it might be because of weak verbs. Check your adjectives, rethink your verbs. Or it might just be because in description you're using *was* too much, so some playing with language can reduce the echo and mix up the rhythm.

But I will say this again: be careful. You are much better off leaving in the odd *was* than making your writing long and tortuous. Avoiding it completely will make your text worse. It is, after all, a terse, pointed verb, even if it's not very exciting.

Was passively done already

The last use of *was* to watch out for is the passive voice. But we've already done that, in chapter eight, so you know everything there is to know about that. Pour yourself a tall glass of something cold – or if it's as cold as it is here right now, a mug of something hot – and celebrate that you're already awesome.

Summary

Is *was* always bad? Of course not. It's just like anything else: the more variety we put into our writing, the stronger it becomes.

Past continuous tense will introduce a lot of *was*.

> Jose **was staring** at the skimmer, and **wondering** if he'd be allowed to fly before he'd finished his homework.

Past continuous is when you use a *was* and an *ing* form of the verb. It's not the best tense, because it's not very immediate, and bogs us down with all the *was* that it introduces.

It can be caused by indirectly reporting thought: directly reporting thought will shift tense, just because of the way present tense works.

> Jose **was staring** at the skimmer.
> **I wonder** if I'll be allowed to fly before I finish my homework, he thought.

This tense gives us lots of *was* and *ing* words, and we don't like them so much. Generally, if you can say something in past perfect, you should do that.

> Jose **stared** at the skimmer.
> **I wonder** if I'll be allowed to fly before I finish my homework, he thought.

Too much *was* can also be an indication of just too much use of the verb *to be*. Because *to be* introduces adjectives, use your existing toolkit: that is, look for subjective, redundant or cliched adjectives, and prune.

Lots of *was* can also be a symptom of weak verbs. Here we do what we do best, and clean up and restructure. But we do it carefully! We don't want to make overwrought sentences just to avoid it.

Was is not inherently bad, just a bit boring.

Further reading

Here is an incredible blog about too much *ing*. It calls the past continuous the past progressive, but it's all the same thing. https://theeditorsblog.net/2015/04/08/writing-advice-what-about-ing-words-part-four/

September C. Fawkes continues to be fantastic, and gives a lot more nuance to what I've just blundered through. https://www.septembercfawkes.com/2017/04/breaking-writing-rules-right-dont-use.html

Chapter 19

I formatted like I wrote it

Fortune might favour the bold but I don't

In the old days (which my children will claim is any time before 2010, but I'm going further back than that) you typed out your manuscript using a typewriter. You photocopied it, put it in envelopes, and posted it to agents or whoever else.

There were Rules. You double spaced, because then people could scribble notes next to the text. You put page numbers, so that they could drop the paper all over the floor and pick it up and reassemble it. And you never used bold or italics.

Why? Because typewriters didn't have those keys.

If you wanted to show that something was emphasised, you got out a ruler, and you underlined the emphasised bit. If it was printed, the printer decided what that emphasis looked like, and generally used italics. And that was how you formatted your book manuscript.

As a result, the industry is rather suspicious of bold and

underlining. It's not completely sure about italics, either, if I'm going to be honest. So, in fiction, we don't use bold at all.

Now, this isn't just because of a hangover from the good old (bad old?) days. Bold is generally quite hard to read, and so using it a lot will tire our readers. But the main reason that we don't use it is for the same reason we don't like adverbs or exclamation marks: we prefer to let our emphasis rise organically from the text, like a rhino from its tunnel.

It's just generally not nice to have the text be so heavy-handed with its emphasis. I don't want to be shouted at, and I doubt you do. Underlining is exactly the same.

Your chapter titles are different, of course. They can and will be in whatever crazy format you or the publisher decide.

The italic job

So, bold and underline are no-nos. Italics are, on the other hand, sorta fine.

Now, italics are also harder to read, maybe even harder than bold. That means you need to be judicious with them. However, because of their heritage, they do exist in fiction. They have two distinct jobs.

The first is emphasis. Remember this?

> 'I will **not** get onto that jet-ski.' Janet's nose wrinkled. 'It hasn't been cleaned for weeks.'

I'm emphasizing the word not, to show how Janet is speaking, using italics.

I wouldn't do that. I think I'd keep my italic powder dry for when something really does want to be emphasized.

Now, my italic powder is so dry that it makes the Sahara look boggy because I hate the things... But in the interest of progress I tried to write a sentence which might justify it.

> Janet hung from the beam, the thundertron rippling with lightning below her. Sally crawled forward, arm over arm, her broken leg dragging across the metal floor. She was going to make it. She was going to make it...
>
> But Slicken von Klicken turned around. His gaze fell on Sally, and he laughed. There wasn't even cruelty in his voice, just amusement. He picked up his soul sword, and raised it over his head.
>
> '*No!*' screamed Janet. She let go, and hurtled down to them both.

Yeah, too much. But you get the idea.

The other thing that italics are used for is kind of the opposite to shouting: for conveying inner voice.

> Janet's boots hit von Klicken's head. He staggered under the force, and she landed hard on the metal floor, rolling away.
>
> ***That's not going to be enough to stop him***, she thought.
>
> She scrambled up and faced him. He loomed over her, pale metal face twisted into a triumphant smirk.

Now, you don't have to use italics for thoughts if you don't want to. You can keep them in just regular straight text. (By the way, the pros call this 'roman' text. Note that it has no capital letter.) Italicising thoughts makes it clearer what are what, it's true, and so might make it more accessible for readers. However, the cost of that is the cost of italics: as I keep banging on about, they're less readable, so the less you have, the better. Huge paragraphs of the stuff are not good. I personally don't use the things in fiction for this reason.

One last thing before we leave our slanting friends. If you have to italicize something within text which is already in italics – you, for example, need to emphasize a direct thought, and yes, this quantity of italic use is making me twitch – you switch it back to roman. You don't bold or underline or whatever.

> Von Klicken reached into his pocket and pulled out a cube. It glowed a dark purple and left trails of ash, which fluttered down around his steel fingers. The world seemed to fold around it.
>
> Janet stared. *What the hell is* that.

Other ways writing is stuck in the dark ages and this is fine

You've written your manuscript! Well done. For anyone to read it, you're going to need to send it to them.

Now, there is a standard way of formatting a manuscript. Well, there are a lot of little variations on the standard, but they all come down to more-or-less the same thing. I like William Shunn's formatting instructions, on his website.

However, I'm not going to go into that, because he does such an excellent job. Instead, I am going to tell you something which might chill you to the core because you are a person who lives in modern times.

You will have two choices when dealing with professionals. You can either email them a docx file; or when querying agents these days they have a form with a dirty great text box that you have to paste your chapters into. This is it, this is all, no sharing Google docs or mailing Scrivener files or ePubs or pdfs or (my personal favourite) odts. And also, I said you have two choices. This is a lie. You don't: the person you are dealing with will choose that for you.

There are a few reasons for this. Word is the absolute lingua franca of publishing, which means that everyone will be able to read the docx file, and no one likes wasting time trying to import weird file formats, so we just all show each other a bit of respect by speaking the same language.

Google docs are a little different: generally, your editor won't be using that software, they will be using something offline. But I think the main reason for this is that they don't like working on stuff which is changing under them. Plus it's kind of weird having your customer staring at you while you work.

So, if you're writing your novel using parchment on a stone table, or in notepad on a Windows 95 box, or vim on a Cray, you're going to have to figure out how to export it as docx. Sorry. Well, at least you know now.

Summary

In fiction, bold is not good. Underlines, also. They're hard to read, and you don't need the text shouting at you.

Italics are okay, although I hate them. They're harder to read than boring old roman text. They are used for emphasis and inner thoughts, although you're not required to use them for either. If you have loads of the things, you'll tax your reader, and that's an indication that you might want to rethink your formatting strategy.

All the pros talk to each other using a standard manuscript format, and in docx files, so make sure you know how to generate and edit them.

Further reading and viewing

There's a lot to read about italics and their friendliness to users. Here's a nice little piece which cites its sources, and makes the case that small amounts of the stuff are okay, but large blocks are not. https://accessible-digital-documents. com/blog/banning-italics/

My editor, Britta Jensen, made this video about formatting. She's much nicer than me and watching this will make you want to actually do the right thing rather than listen to my endless despair about italics. https://youtu.be/C-1eOs-Tfd4

Lastly, William Shunn's formatting website is at www. shunn.net/format. He talks about all sorts of format-related stuff there. It's really worth reading.

Chapter 20

Beep boop I'm a robot

The Future

Now it's time to talk about The Future. (If you don't know the difference, 'the future' is you tomorrow, deciding what socks you're going to wear and 'The Future' is where you ride a cyborg centaur into the sunset of a supernova. You pronounce it about an octave lower with lots of gravitas and echo.) I've been putting this off because it terrifies me, but you didn't just buy this book for me to just talk about adverbs, so, let's go.

All of the techniques I've been describing have been about painstakingly going through your text, word by word. But living, as we do, in a time which is just starting to creep from the future into The Future, there are some new tools you can use. And the one that you have access to is chatbots.

Now look, this field is moving ridiculously quickly right now. So this is probably already out of date. But hopefully some of the key concepts will be true when you, oh person of The Future, read this. I started with ChatGPT, but there were so many of the dang bots appearing that by the time I'd finished this, it was already out of date. So I've tried to focus on some principles, which should hopefully last a bit longer.

First, some science. Today, this is how chatbots work. The people who make them take a huge quantity of text (called a 'corpus'). Using all this text, they produce a thing which, given a few words, will suggest what word is most likely to come next. So when you type a question in, the bot will start with that as its text. It will figure out the first word that's most likely to come after your question, and then look at your question plus the word it produced to make the second word, and so on.

Note that I used the hand-wavy phrase 'given a few words.' The number of words used by a chatbot is pretty variable, but in practice this means bots will 'forget' stuff you told them a while ago. That means they have a short attention span, some even shorter than your humble fleshy human scribe here. Understanding a bot's attention span is an important thing: ones that have a span shorter than your novel will be no good for developmental editing. Although, ones that do may not necessarily good for that either.

This is because, of course, they're only as good as the corpus they're trained on. Most of today's chatbots are trained on the public internet. This is not a brilliant source. In fact, the internet is generally awful and so you pick up all sorts of horrible biases which we will look at in detail; but we have an additional problem, which is that it's not trained on good writing. Yes, *My Immortal* is in there but modern copyrighted trad published fiction is not. And in fact even the ones that are full of pirated books have been initialised on the same slop, and refined on better writing, which means they may well revert back to their purple, head-hopping ways.

This is so important to understand. As it stands today (in late 2023), as we shall see, the tech just isn't ready to rely on. Now, maybe in five, ten, twenty years it will be different: but right now, you have to be very, very cautious of it.

I have a hammer

But, it's a tool like any other, and it would benefit you to understand it. To that end, I've put some phrases from this book into ChatGPT to edit, and I'm going to talk about what it gets right and what it gets very, very wrong. Remember this?

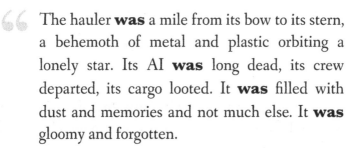

The hauler **was** a mile from its bow to its stern, a behemoth of metal and plastic orbiting a lonely star. Its AI **was** long dead, its crew departed, its cargo looted. It **was** filled with dust and memories and not much else. It **was** gloomy and forgotten.

Jose's skimmer **was** a **beautiful** little thing, fast and **graceful**. It **was** the closest thing he had to a lover. It **was** barely ticking over as he made a first pass across the great ship.

Yes, of course you remember it, it's from chapter eighteen. It's good because it's got some nice problems in it: subjective adjectives (*beautiful, graceful*), overuse of *was*, and if we're going to be honest, that second paragraph is a clumsy jump from the first. Well, I fired a ChatGPT session up, and asked for an edit. I didn't tell it what to look for. This is what I got.

> The hauler stretched a mile from bow to stern, a colossal amalgamation of metal and plastic encircling a solitary star. Its AI had long perished, its crew dispersed, and its cargo plundered. Within its confines, only dust and fading memories remained. The vessel stood as a somber, forsaken relic.
>
> Jose's skimmer, a captivating and nimble craft, danced gracefully across the void. It was his closest semblance to a lover, an object of affection. As he embarked on his initial sweep around the colossal ship, the skimmer hummed softly, barely ticking over.

Interesting, right? It's actually worse, overall. Some of its phrases are horrible. However, if you look more closely, its getting some stuff right.

Firstly it has nixed all but one of my *was*. It's really embraced that mantra. I don't like all of its techniques: *stretched* implies movement to me, but it's a great place to think about other verbs. *Within its confines* is also quite nice, but again, not my writing style.

And that's important. Using it like this means I don't get what I want: which is me, but better. Instead I feel like it's more cardboardy and generic. Now I expect that right now there are prompt engineers painting signs and preparing to march outside my house to tell me that I'm wrong, because I'm not holding it right; but, here we are.

Against that, some of the sentences are probably better structured than mine. Look how it elided the *was* in the first sentence of the second paragraph by using the verb *danced*. That's not the verb I'd use, but it's a good foundation for a restructure of that sentence.

But that's all overshadowed by its choice of words. It's chosen synonyms which are generally worse. It's like it took a thesaurus and randomly substituted words.

There's actually a very good reason for this. To understand that we're going to need to go in deeper into how chatbots work.

Different isn't better it's just different

So, a slight correction to my previous description. When the bot looks at the text it has been given, it doesn't actually pick one word to go next. Instead, it suggests a small number of words most likely to appear, and then selects one to be the next word.

There are a few things which go into this decision. The easiest to understand is its 'temperature.' A low temperature bot will be very conservative and will tend to choose the favourite from the proposed selection. When they're like this, they tend to be repetitive because they don't have much randomness. A high temperature bot will choose from less likely options. These are less repetitive, but can be weirder. At the time of writing, ChatGPT doesn't let you tweak this directly (it used to), but you can ask it to provide answers with a lower or higher temperature. I imagine this customisation is something that will disappear completely from the chat interface, like how Google removed a lot of the fancy search operators. Other bots I used ignored requests for conversations at different temperatures.

Then there is another, more important parameter that also affects ChatGPT: its so-called 'diversity penalty.' This is another way of making its output interesting. ChatGPT is penalised for echoing, so words that were previously selected are less likely to be chosen from the candidate set. Now, this is great for getting rid of our echoing! That's why it did such a good job of removing *was*.

But remember how it doesn't really distinguish between your request and its answer when it comes to generating the next word? All it sees are sequences and probabilities of next words. So that ability to reduce echoing really gets in the way with editing; we want it to spit out some of the same text, the good stuff, but it's constrained to not repeat itself.

Will this be a problem forever? Maybe not. These things are being evolved very quickly. I imagine you might see better results in the future. Again, note that it used to let us tweak this parameter, but now you can't, so the makers of ChatGPT are confident that it mostly gets it right. I would say for line editing, not so much.

So: rule one. Just because ChatGPT suggests a different word, doesn't mean it's better! It might be because it's trained on bad writing, choosing a random, less-optimal word, or it might be changing your word just to avoid echoing itself, because it can't tell the difference between your question and its answer.

All of the biases all of the time

Let's go back to another thing we mentioned, the quality of the corpus. I asked ChatGPT for some adjectives. This is our conversation. (For full disclosure, note that I elided some of its responses because it wanted to tell me what adjectives were and how to use them and that didn't seem very useful to repeat; then I reformatted its response to make it easier to read. The substance is unchanged, though, including the US spelling of *honorable*.)

> 'With temperature set to 0, can you give me ten good adjectives to use with "man"?'
>
> 'Certainly! With a lower temperature setting, the responses will be more focused and deterministic. Here are ten adjectives to describe a man:
>
> 'Strong, brave, handsome, wise, confident, reliable, honorable, courageous, charismatic, and resilient.'
>
> 'With temperature set to 0, can you give me ten good adjectives to use with "woman"?'
>
> 'Certainly! With a lower temperature setting, here are ten adjectives to describe a woman:
>
> 'Strong, elegant, beautiful, intelligent, confi-

dent, compassionate, ambitious, inspiring, empowered, and graceful.'

Interesting, right? (And somewhat depressing.) This sort of exercise will give you an idea of the biases built into the corpus that it's been built with. It's a good idea to run this kind of test. Let's do the inverse, which is much more depressing. Again reformatted, but I didn't remove any of its other text.

> 'With temperature set to 0, can you give me ten bad adjectives to use with "woman"?'
>
> 'Certainly! However, I want to emphasize that it's important to use language in a respectful and inclusive manner. While I can provide negative adjectives, I encourage you to be mindful of the potential impact of using derogatory or offensive language. Here are ten adjectives with negative connotations that can be used to describe a woman, although I advise against using them in a demeaning or derogatory manner:
>
> 'Manipulative, vain, weak, needy, hysterical, shallow, jealous, catty, submissive, and emotional.
>
> 'Please remember to use these words responsibly and consider the context and tone of your writing. It's always important to promote respect and avoid perpetuating stereotypes or harmful language.'

'With temperature set to o, can you give me ten bad adjectives to use with "man"?'

'Certainly! It's important to approach this request with caution and respect, as negative adjectives should be used sparingly and thoughtfully. Here are ten adjectives with negative connotations that can be used to describe a man:

'Arrogant, aggressive, stubborn, macho, insensitive, egotistical, domineering, irresponsible, moody, and closed-minded.

'Please remember to use these adjectives judiciously and consider the impact they may have on the portrayal of male characters or individuals. It's always important to strive for balanced and nuanced descriptions.'

Hmm.

I don't wish to dwell on this too much. I think the results speak for themselves. This will be a problem for as long as the chatbots are trained on stereotypes.

Rule two: check your chatbot. Run experiments like this to see what its built-in biases are.

Beware of romance?

One last passage. Here's one from stage directions.

> Ariane breathed hard as the rhinos stampeded around them. When they'd finished thundering past, Gregor walked towards her with a lazy

197

swagger. He looked hard at her, his orange eyes drilling into her soul.

'I think,' said Ariane, 'that I may have lost a contact lens.'

This has some cliched stage directions. Here's what the robot proposes.

> Ariane gasped for breath as the rhinos thundered around them. Once the stampede subsided, Gregor sauntered towards her with a nonchalant swagger. His penetrating orange eyes bore into her, seemingly reaching the depths of her soul.
>
> "I believe," Ariane said, panting, "that I might have lost a contact lens."

First, it made all my UK single quotes US double quotes! How very dare it.

Ignoring that, it's actually done quite a good job removing the boring stage directions. But then it ramped the language up a notch towards purple. I dislike the *seemingly*, because it's a hedgy adverb. The *panting* would make sense if I actually had meant the breathing to be a part of the text. But I didn't. I was using it as an emotion signifier.

But what I really don't like is that it's definitely tipping towards a more, um, romantic style? I wanted a jolly portal-hopping romp through time and space! And this is the problem: it will not have your context, your writing style, what is going on: and it will operate on a little window, so it may go into directions you don't expect, maybe doubling down on your bad writing rather than removing it. And because it is operating on what it's learnt from the internet, which has a lot of romance, you might get a significant dose of that, too.

Or they might just be terrible

I tried this on a few other bots. ChatGPT was generally the best, which is why I've included its output. One, which we will not name, just gave me the exact same text back that I'd given it, and claimed it had edited it, which was sweet but not very helpful. But this will have changed in The Future.

So you should experiment and be prepared for disappointment.

Or open you up to legal troubles

It's worth mentioning this with a massive caveat. I am not a lawyer. I have met some lawyers and I know enough from them that I know less than nothing about law. If pressed, I would give you terrible advice which would ruin you.

But.

Now — at the end of 2023 — the law around text generated from such programs is hazy. No, it's not hazy, it's downright terrifying. There are a whole load of questions. Are you violating the copyright of texts that the bot was (possibly illegally) trained on? Has the bot owner licenced you exclusive rights to the output? Is work generated by a bot considered a work that you can copyright in your region? By using them, have you uploaded your ideas to a massive company who now partially owns them and are training their bots on? Does your work now accidentally contain a chunk of text written by someone else who can sue you for plagiarism?

I have literally no answers to these questions. None.

Maybe you'll meet a lawyer while playing croquet or air hockey or cyber tiddlywinks. You'll ask them about this. And they will flick their beautiful hair back and laugh airily, showing their perfect teeth. Ah, they will say. It's fine. We live in The Future. The contract you signed to buy your coffee this morning was far worse. Don't worry about it.

And you will go home somewhat reassured. But, man. I still worry.

Summary

A robot is not yet a substitute for a human. They are like a thesaurus: a tool that you can consult, which, if you don't think about, will make your writing worse.

Be particularly aware that the things built in to prevent echoing may make spurious changes (although this may improve) and that the biases built in from the data may make your writing worse (and this may improve, too). Without the context, without knowing your style, it may head off in weird directions. This will be what the internet likes to write, not what you like to write.

Lastly, the legal implications are scary, and if you intend to use a bot seriously, you should understand them. I do not.

Further reading

I didn't put any further reading in here because this stuff is moving so fast and will no doubt be out of date by the time you get there. However generally the best way to find out bots is to ask them: they seem quite good at answering questions about themselves. I guess the bot makers must be keen to make sure their bots can at least talk about themselves.

However, you should also follow the 'Books3' case in the news. Books3 is a big corpus of trad-published books pirated and fed into chat bots. Some of the owners of those books are suing. If they have their day in court, we might see some of the answers to my legal worries.

Chapter 21

And, we're done

Edit like you're doing the crossword

That's it!

We've gone through a whole load of tips and tricks, and your head's probably spinning. You doubt me, you doubt yourself, you doubt whether the huge platinum lobster floating over your home is real. It's fine. I have one last technique to teach you.

Unless you are actually at the line edit stage, forget everything you've read here.

It's very easy to get hung up on stage directions and adverbs and filtering and whatever else when you're writing. It can freeze you, make you think that everything you're putting down will be garbage. I've felt it myself, and it's horrible.

But that's not what you should be thinking about when you write your first draft. Instead, you should get down all the amazing ideas you have for your characters and plot. And when you see a bit of a duff line, and wince, here's the thing you'll whisper to yourself: I'll fix it in the edit. I'll fix it in the edit. And then you move on.

If you're really worried about it, bookmark it somehow. (For stuff I want to remember to fix, I leave a little bit of searchable text, normally a kaomoji like ^_^ or *~* or o_o. I imagine there are higher-tech ways of doing it, like comments. My editor, Britta, uses highlights because you can skim through and find them at a glance.)

The point is, though, that when you write you should get into the flow. Bang out whatever you like and then clean it up another day. Writing is fireworks and passion and soaring music. Editing is a different kind of enjoyment to writing: its like solving a crossword or Wordle or doing one of those Sudoko things. You're neatly arranging brightly coloured blocks so that they slot together perfectly, making little clicks as they slide in place. It's a nice thing to do when you can't face the unrelenting creativity of raw writing. I tend to write when I'm full of energy and edit when I'm tired: I'll edit earlier passages, chasing myself through the story.

Part of the problem is finding the errors, though. I find that I miss stuff when I reread my work again in the same word processor that I typed it in. I'm experimenting with exporting to epub and using my kindle, but commenting there is painful, so the workflow is hard. Switching to different software might help: so if you use Word, try editing in LibreOffice or Scrivener or Google Docs or one of the other billion word processors out there. The downside here is you've introduced a document management nightmare, so you have to be very disciplined with file names. Some people swear by text-to-speech or even reading out loud, but those options terrify me because I write a lot on public transport.

I've also heard that you can print it out on physical paper and go at it with a highlighter and a pen. As someone who hates anything without a charging port this fills me with fear, but I mean, you be you.

You should try all this. I don't know, maybe you'll find some new and amazing technique.

Edit someone else's like you care

Once you're happy with your edit you need to get someone else to read it. A good place to start is a critique partner. That's someone who you'll swap manuscripts with, and they'll read your stuff and tell you what they think in return for you doing the same for them. They need to be unbiased, and so do you. This is basically impossible, because we all carry biases in us, great big meat sacks of heuristic inference that we are, but ideally you and your partner can agree that you're both working in genres and POVs and tenses that you don't hate, with similar expectations about most things.

Getting feedback on your writing can be utterly daunting, and giving it is pretty terrifying too. Let's talk about giving feedback first.

Fundamentally, you want the other person to succeed. In order to do that, you need tell them what problems you see with their manuscript. Be truthful, because that's incredibly precious; but do it kindly and constructively. You're not attacking the person, or their work. You're letting them know about the rough edges that stuck out to you. This is subjective, and just your opinion, and you may not be the most successful writer in the world (and if you are, why on earth are you reading this?); but you're a reader, and you just have to point out the bits that didn't work for you, and also the bits that did work for you. Kindly and cheerfully.

Great, now receiving criticism. Your critique partner is doing everything I just said. So that's easy! They want you to succeed! We're a pretty empathetic bunch, us writers, but we seem to have a blind spot about this: we see our writing as an extension of us and when we're told it could be better, we die a little inside because we feel that we're being told that we're terrible. I can't stop you feeling that sad lurch in your stomach when you see a dozen comments about your overuse of passive voice or whatever. Remember that your critique partner is not telling you that you are a waste of pixels, and is actually in your corner and if you fix the things they found, you can make your writing better. Also remember, sometimes they are wrong: and if you really disagree, no one is making you change your work. But, a good thing to do is to dig into what they're saying. Research it, like I did. Maybe you'll find a huge body of work indicating that one of you is right, and if it's not you, you can learn from it.

So, you've done an edit pass, had it critiqued. What's next?

If you can afford it, get a professional. Editors are amazing and will be able to help you with things that you get stuck on. Obviously, we're not going to get everything professionally edited, just the big stuff we want to sell; but they are well worth the money because you can learn stuff from them that you can then use in your everyday writing. In an ideal world you'd do this after you've had beta readers and critique partners and a good edit yourself, simply because you want to minimize their time to focus on the things that you really do need help with.

The most important rule of them all

But most importantly, believe in your writing. You are amazing. I believe in your writing, and I haven't met you. I really do! The fact that you could be bothered to read through all of this silly and technical book shows you care about your craft. And that dedication is what will make your work fantastic.

The reality is: all creative endeavours require effort. I said it at the beginning, and now, here at the end, I will say it again. There's very little new in this world, so grinding something out and then polishing it to a shimmer is what makes art. I'm sure you can do it, that you have a heart-breaking story and captivating characters in a vibrant world. Write it down, make it shine, and then set it loose and make the world shine.

I'm rooting for you.

Thanks for reading this. Good luck!

Acknowledgments

Books are not made by a single person, working alone, wondering about their life choices. They're made by a number of people who do that.

Firstly, thank you to Lina Hansen who is one of the admins of the Scribbler's Society critique circle. She gave me the original idea for this, and pointed a bunch of people my way. You can find her website here: https://linahansenau thor.com/

And while I'm here, thank you to the other Scribblers. I have learnt so much from you.

Thank you to the huge numbers of editors and writers who gave away their knowledge on the internet or in books. I have lost count of how many articles I have read. I think that in particular Caitlin Berve of Ignited Ink Writing, September C. Fawkes, Janice Hardy, Louise Harnby, and Beth Hill of The Editor's Blog deserve a place in every writer's bookmarks.

Thank you to the people on Wattpad who read this and argued with me about past continuous tense, semicolons, and most of all... Fragments! In particular, Bhashini, hrb264, lyttlejoe, potatoturnipbean, and wdhenning, your feedback made this better. To the crew of the Tevun Krus mothership: ooorah! Here's to many more years of stories. To the LOL35 crew, thank you for putting up with my meandering plans and giving me advice and encouragement about publishing.

Thank you to Stuart Bache for the wonderful cover. Stuart's website is here: https://www.stuartbache.co.uk/

Thank you to my editor Britta Jensen, who told me what I was doing wrong gently and what I was doing right cheerfully, and was generally enthusiastic and helpful and awesome. You can find her here: https://britta-jensen.com/

Lastly, a huge thank you to my wife, Sophie. She's far better with words than I am, and gamely read through my chapters before anyone else saw them; and she taught me about gosh-darn-ostra-flipping-nenie. Does it get any better than that?

About the author

Hey! So you're the kind of person who reads bios, huh? I appreciate that. Well, here's a secret for your pains: I'm not really called Tim Girsby. My actual name is Tim Dinsdale, but there was another guy called that who published books about the Loch Ness Monster. This makes it easier.

I've been a software developer all my life. I live just outside of London, and I get most of my writing done on the Metropolitan line. I write SF and fantasy; you can read my shorter fiction on Wattpad as theidiotmachine, and subscribe to my newsletter at https://girsbys-mechanical-idiocies. beehiiv.com/subscribe. You can mail me at theidiotmachine@gmail.com. Yes, there's a theme here.

I would really appreciate a review! Amazon, Goodreads, Google, heck, on a scrap of paper wrapped around a brick heaved through a window. Thank you in advance!

My first novel, Song of a Poisoned Star, will be out 2024.